John Nevins Andrews

FLAME for the LORD

John Nevins Andrews

FLAME for the LORD

Virgil Robinson

Previously printed under the title
J. N. Andrews, Prince of Scholars

TEACH Services, Inc.
P U B L I S H I N G
www.TEACHServices.com • (800) 367-1844

Facsimile Reproduction

As this book played a formative role in the development of Christian thought and the publisher feels that this book, with its candor and depth, still holds significance for the church today. Therefore the publisher has chosen to reproduce this historical classic from an original copy. Frequent variations in the quality of the print are unavoidable due to the condition of the original. Thus the print may look darker or lighter or appear to be missing detail, more in some places than in others.

Copyright © 2004, 2015 TEACH Services, Inc.
ISBN-13: 978-1-57258-283-5
Library of Congress Control Number: 2004105691

Published by

TEACH Services, Inc.
P U B L I S H I N G
www.TEACHServices.com • (800) 367-1844

CONTENTS

BOYHOOD DAYS

"HAVE A care, Pa. You know they haven't caught King Philip. I do not think the Indians are going to give us a moment's peace until their leader is either killed or captured." *

Ezra Andrews kissed his wife's upturned face.

"Don't worry, Eliza. There hasn't been an attack in this area for many months."

Ezra took his hat from the table and his musket down from the rack. Each of his four sons did the same. Walking out to the tool shed, each man took up a hoe and went to the cornfield. Stacking their muskets against a stone wall, they began cultivating the long rows of shoulder-high corn.

Unknown to the Andrews men, many sharp eyes had been spying on their home and that field since dawn. Waiting until the men had reached the far end of the field, a band of Indians rushed out of the forest, cutting between them and their weapons.

Ezra and his sons dashed for the forest to seek protection among the trees. But more Indians were wait-

---

* Some of the conversations in this book are imaginary but in keeping with the spirit of the events described.

ing for them there. In desperation the men yanked small trees out of the ground to use as weapons as they tried to force their way through the ranks of their attackers. But it was hopeless from the beginning. One by one they were pierced by arrows or struck down by tomahawks until all five of them were dead.

The war cries of the Indians and the shouts of her husband and her sons, alerted Eliza to the situation in the cornfield. Looking out the door, she stood rooted to the spot in horror as she saw her men fall one by one to the ground. She fully expected the Indians to attack the house, but evidently the savages had accomplished their purpose, for the shouting died away.

A period of silence convinced her that the Indians had left. Quickly she went out into the field, where she found her husband and sons were all dead. Only a younger brother, Peter, escaped the hand of the enemy. He had stayed in bed that morning, too ill to take his accustomed place in the field with his brothers. Now only he and his sister, Mary, and their mother, Eliza, remained of the large family that had surrounded the breakfast table an hour earlier.

Peter Andrews grew up and married, becoming the father of a large family of sons. Years passed. The Andrews family spread over many parts of New England. When the American Revolution broke out, among the patriots who fought and suffered with General George Washington's army were David Andrews, a descendant of Peter, and his friend John Nevins.

Half a century later, Sarah, the granddaughter of John Nevins, married Edward, a grandson of David Andrews. This couple settled in the village of Poland, Maine. There, on July 22, 1829, a son was born, whom they named John Nevins, after his great-grandfather. Two years later his brother, William, was born. There were daughters also, but their names have not been recorded.

While John Nevins Andrews was still small the family moved to Paris, a town built on the top and sides of a long, gentle hill about thirty miles from Poland. Here Edward built a house for his family, and here his children grew up. Paris Hill, as the community is called today, is smaller than it was a century ago. In those days it was the headquarters of Paris township.

The Andrews family were devoutly religious people. One Sunday they went to church as usual. The speaker for the day was a minister by the name of Daniel B. Randall. He began his sermon by reading a verse from the book of Revelation: "And I saw a great white throne, and him that sat on it, from whose face the earth and the heaven fled away; and there was found no place for them" (chap. 20:11). These solemn words made a profound impression on 5-year-old John. The thought that he would someday stand before that great white throne sent shivers down his spine.

When Sarah Andrews felt that John was old enough to understand the significance of joining the church she took him to the Methodist meetinghouse, where he was baptized and his name was enrolled in the church record book. In the fall of the year she took him to the little schoolhouse and enrolled him as a student.

School was a delight to John. Early in life he made it a practice to rise at four o'clock in the morning and spend two or three hours before breakfast studying the Bible and praying.

But life was not all books for him. He joined his schoolmates in the usual sports. In summer he would take his rod and go to the lake with his companions, often returning with a string of fresh fish for his mother to fry for the family. In the winter sleds and toboggans came out, and the boys spent many happy hours racing down the snowy slopes of nearby hills. The bitter cold of the New England winters turned the sparkling waters of its lakes to smooth ice. So there were skating parties on the icy ponds and rivers.

Life was not easy at the home of Edward Andrews. As was true of most New England farms, the fields were liberally sprinkled with stones of all sizes. The ground was shallow and the soil poor. Farmer Andrews never enjoyed good health, and his two sons were both under par physically. In fact, John later wrote: "I never saw the time when my physical strength was fully equal to that of most of those youth of my years." His brother was a cripple and able to do little.

At the age of 11, having acquired a working knowledge of the three R's, John was forced to quit school because of poor health. From that time on whatever he learned he taught himself. Wherever he went he carried a book. Whenever there was a spare moment, no matter how brief, he would pull out his book and seek to absorb a few ideas from its pages.

Loving the Bible as he did, he naturally wished to read it in the languages in which it had been originally written. At his request his father got books in Greek, Latin, and Hebrew, which John studied diligently. One by one he mastered those languages. Before his death he was able to read the Bible in seven languages.

Edward Andrews had a brother, Charles, who was extremely prosperous. Charles, who also made his home in Paris Hill, was a Member of Congress while

John was growing up. When Government duties kept Uncle Charles in Washington, his wife often returned to New England during the summer to escape the sweltering heat of the capital. It was only natural that she should visit in the home of her brother-in-law.

In a letter to her husband she described his nephews as follows: "At Edward Andrews' they have only two sons. The older one (John) a perfect gentleman by nature, and a fine scholar."

At about that time John and his family attended a series of lectures given by a minister on the subject of the soon return of Christ. Father Andrews carefully looked up the verses on this subject as quoted by the visitor. Since what this minister taught agreed with the Bible, Andrews and his family accepted the new doctrine. They thus became members of the group of Millerites, as those people were called who accepted the teachings of William Miller. Those who rejected the teachings of Miller took every opportunity to oppose and ridicule those who accepted what came to be called the Advent message.

It was customary for the Adventists to meet to sing and pray together. One evening as John and an elderly friend, a Mr. Davis, were on their way to a meeting, a group of rowdies appeared and tried to block their path and turn them back. The leader of this band carried a heavy whip and advanced on Davis, with the intention of showering blows upon him. John Andrews stepped forward and placed himself in front of his companion. The gang leader motioned him to step out of the way.

"It says in the Bible that we are to carry one another's burdens," John said. "If you are going to whip Mr. Davis, you must whip me too."

Shamed by this unexpected act of courage, the leader tucked his whip under his arm, bowed his head, and indicated that the two might proceed.

"It is too bad to whip a boy," he muttered as they passed.

Summer and winter, John continued doing a man's work with his father on the farm. It was hard work, and when mealtime came he was always very hungry. Years later he was to speak of his intemperance in eating as a youth. He was to receive a testimony from Ellen White pointing out that he would be able to work better if he ate less. But this was long before John heard of Mrs. White, and he partook heartily of the food his mother prepared.

A typical breakfast at the Andrews home began with corn-meal or oatmeal porridge, followed by fried eggs with bacon or sausages. Fried potatoes, hot biscuits with butter, jelly, or jam, mince, apple, or pumpkin pie, doughnuts and cheese, fruit sauce, apples, and coffee were also served. Coffee was always drunk, with plenty of cream and sugar.

Dinners were as lavish as breakfasts. Suppers were not far behind. Baked beans were served every day. At dinnertime, cake took the place of pie. The dinner roast leftovers were served as cold cuts for supper. And should one become hungry between meals, a full cooky jar always stood in plain view on the pantry shelf. Near bedtime further snacks could be had in the form of hickory nuts, apples, popcorn, taffy, and cider. John did not realize in those days that such intemperate eating could lay a foundation for years of poor health.

By the time he was 14 John was recognized as a powerful spiritual leader. He was often invited to address the people of Paris on the subject of religion. As he continued his deep study of the Bible he became more and more sure that Christ would return sometime in 1843 or 1844.

Those years came and went, and Jesus did not come. John, with thousands of other Adventists, was bitterly disappointed. But he refused to surrender his hope, and continued to study the Bible in order to discover why the people had not been taken to heaven by Jesus.

Other Adventist scholars all over New England were trying to solve the mystery. One of these, Hiram Edson, of New York State, wrote in an Adventist pamphlet an article proving that on the day of the disappointment, October 22, 1844, Jesus had gone from the holy place in the heavenly sanctuary into the Most Holy Place to begin His ministry there.

Another writer, T. M. Preble, who had worked with Miller and other Millerite leaders, wrote a tract urging that Christians should keep the seventh day of the week as the Sabbath and not Sunday, the first.

A copy of Preble's tract was sent to a Mr. Stowell, one of the Paris Adventists. He glanced at it and laid it down. His 15-year-old daughter, Marian, picked it up and read it with interest. Its message seemed so true and convincing that she showed it to her brother, Oswald. He also was convinced that the seventh day is the true Sabbath.

"What are we going to do about it?" Oswald asked.

"I think we ought to keep it," was Marian's reply.

On Friday the two young people tried to do all of their next day's work, as well as their regular duties. If their parents noticed anything different in this, they made no comment.

"I wonder what John Andrews would say about this," remarked Oswald to his sister on Sunday. "If anyone knows what the Bible teaches about the Sabbath, it should be John."

So Marian gave the tract to young Andrews and

asked him to read it. John was at first shocked by what it taught.

"Is it possible," he asked himself, "that all these years we have been doing wrong in keeping Sunday?" He began looking up the Bible texts listed by Preble. The deeper he studied, the more certain he became that the Sabbath is the seventh day of the week. He took the tract back to Marian and asked her, "Have your father and mother read this?"

"No, but I have, and so has Oswald. We find we have not been keeping the right Sabbath. What do you think, John?"

"I think the seventh day is the Sabbath. If we think that, Marian, we must keep it."

"Oswald and I did last week. We'll be glad to have you join us. Would you like to take Elder Preble's tract to your parents?"

John took the tract home and persuaded his parents to read it. As a result, the Stowell and Andrews families both kept the next Sabbath together. Other families joined them, and soon quite a company in and around Paris Hill were keeping God's true Sabbath.

I wonder whether many other Christians are keeping the Bible Sabbath, thought John Andrews to himself. To find out, he wrote the publishers of Preble's tract and learned that there was a small company in New Bedford, and another in Washington, New Hampshire.

"I believe this is a Bible truth and that it should be preached everywhere," said John. "May God send us a leader."

God already had a leader prepared, and John was soon to meet him. His name was James White.

INTO the BATTLE

THE SMALL company of Sabbathkeepers in Paris increased steadily during the next years. There were members in South Paris and West Paris, but the majority lived on Paris Hill. Since they were too poor to own a meetinghouse of their own, they met in private homes.

One warm September afternoon a horse and buggy drove up in front of the home of Edward Andrews. Sarah stepped outside to see who was calling. The driver stood up and carefully stepped down onto the ground.

"Why, Charles!" Mrs. Andrews exclaimed. "We didn't know you were coming! Is Hanna with you?"

"Yes, she is over at the house. Congress has recessed until after the elections, so I've come home. I would like to talk with John if he's here. Hanna has told me what a fine young man he has become. From what she says, it is evident that he is a real scholar."

"Yes, he loves his books. You'll find him mowing in the south pasture. I know he will be glad to see you."

So Charles Andrews took the path that led to the pasture. There he found John, scythe in hand, cutting the tall grass to provide hay for the animals during the approaching winter. John greeted his uncle affectionately. He laid down his scythe, and the two men sat in the shade of an apple tree.

"It's good to see you, John," said Charles. "Let's see, you're 17 now, aren't you?"

"That's right, Uncle Charles. My birthday was two months ago."

"What are your plans for the future?"

"I have decided to become a minister."

Uncle Charles frowned. "There are worse professions, but again there are better ones. I have heard a rumor that you are observing the seventh day of the week just as the Jews do. Surely you don't intend to preach that doctrine."

"Uncle Charles, since I am convinced that the seventh day is the only true Sabbath, I must preach it." Both men were silent for a few moments.

"Look, John, I've got something much bigger and better than that for you. With that wonderful mind of yours, you should study law and plan a political career. I'm getting old and won't be running for public office after a couple more terms. There's no reason why you shouldn't go to law school, practice for a while, then run for my seat in Congress. Did you know that more than half the members are lawyers? You could have a brilliant future."

"Uncle Charles," John replied, "I cannot tell you how alluring your suggestion is. But I see two obstacles. First, my health isn't too good. Second, my father is a poor man, and William isn't able to help him much on the farm. A lot of responsibility rests on me."

"If it is finances that are worrying you, that is a problem easily solved." Charles leaned forward and placed his hand on John's shoulder.

"You can choose any university you wish—Harvard, Dartmouth, Yale. I'll arrange your acceptance and pay every bill."

There was another period of silence as John looked for the most tactful way to turn down his uncle's offer without hurting his feelings. Perhaps to postpone making a decision would be the simplest way, he decided.

"Let me think about it, Uncle. You see, whatever decision I now make could change my whole life."

"Very good, John. When you have decided which university you prefer just let me know, and I'll secure your admission. I know your folks are hard up, so I'll agree to buy your clothing. I see a brilliant career ahead for you. But if you go preaching for those Sabbatarians no one will ever hear of you."

So Uncle Charles walked back to the house that day leaving a young man deep in thought. But John had already made up his mind. He had committed his life to proclaiming God's truth, and he was not going to turn back. That night he talked with his parents and told them his decision. Both of them approved.

Two more years passed, and many troubles came to the Sabbathkeepers in Paris. Not a few of their difficulties arose because they had no leader. When they met for services anyone who had a burden to speak rose and talked. Sometimes fanatics would proclaim strange doctrines. For example, one man said that the six thousand years for work ended in 1844. Now they were in the Sabbath of rest, and it was wrong for anyone to work or to plan for the future.

"What nonsense is this?" asked John Andrews scornfully. "If nobody works, who is going to put food into our mouths and clothes on our backs?"

The man stood and pointed his finger toward the ceiling.

"The Lord will provide," he replied solemnly.

"Besides, what do you know about it? You are only a youth."

"The Lord provides indeed, but only for those who do their part," John answered.

Other fanatics came. They quoted from Matthew where Jesus is recorded as telling His disciples they would have to be humble like little children if they wanted to enter the kingdom of heaven. So, to show how humble they were, these fanatics went around on their hands and knees. They ate their food sitting on the floor or behind a door. Other strange doctrines were also taught. The believers became discouraged, and many of them stopped attending Sabbath meetings.

Fifty miles away, at Topsham, Maine, James and Ellen White were staying in the home of Stockbridge Howland. In vision, the Lord showed Mrs. White the troubles in the church in Paris and gave her a message for the fanatics.

She told her husband and Brother Howland about it, and they agreed to take her to Paris. When they arrived a large meeting of all believers was called. Ellen White gave her testimony and reproved those who were making so much trouble.

After one man had interrupted Mrs. White many times, trying to confuse the believers, the Spirit of God came on Stockbridge Howland. He stood up and walked over to face the fanatic. Pointing his finger at him he shouted, "You have torn the hearts of God's children and made them bleed. Leave His house or God will smite you!"

The man reached for his hat, sprang to his feet, and rushed out of the meetinghouse. With the interrupter gone, the people could listen to the instruction God was sending them. God's Spirit came upon them. Confessions were made by parents to children and by children to their parents. John Andrews rose and exclaimed with deep feeling, "I would exchange a thousand errors for one truth."

It was at this meeting that John Andrews publicly took his stand to work for the truth loved and proclaimed by James and Ellen White and Joseph Bates. He was just 20 years old.

Another year passed. Then one day a horse and buggy drove up to the Andrews home. Elder and Mrs. White stepped out. Mrs. Andrews welcomed them warmly and invited them into the house. James White came directly to the point.

"We are looking for a better place to print our paper," he explained. "I've heard there is a printing shop here in Paris. After writing in Rocky Hill, Connecticut, and walking several miles to a print shop in Middletown, I have decided I could save a lot of time by living nearer to a press. So I would like to live in Paris and print our paper here."

"Why not?" replied Mrs. Andrews. "Mr. Mellen's print shop burned down last year, but he has rebuilt it. I'm sure he would be glad for your business. I have plenty of room for you to stay right here with us."

So the Whites moved into the Andrews home that day and remained with them for about half a year. It was in Paris that James White changed the name of his paper from *Present Truth* to a much longer name, the *Second Advent Review and Sabbath Herald,* today commonly called the *Review.* The first number came off the press in November, 1850.

It was in Paris that a publishing committee was set up. Its members consisted of James White, Joseph Bates, S. W. Rhodes, and John N. Andrews. Most of the early articles were about the Sabbath, some long ones dealt with the history of Sunday and how it came to take the place of the Bible Sabbath. Although many of these articles were unsigned, it is evident that John Andrews, with his broad knowledge of church and secular history, wrote them.

Thus began a friendship between James White and John Andrews that was to remain firm and strong for more than thirty years. The relationship between these two men has been compared to that of the apostle Paul and his convert Timothy.

As long as he lived John Andrews wrote articles for the *Review and Herald.* Between 1855 and 1883, he was listed as one of the editors of the paper. He served on the publishing committee for many years.

But John Andrews was not satisfied merely to write articles about the Sabbath. In his heart there burned a great desire to preach.

Only in heaven can a record be found of the travels of young John Andrews during the next five years. The youthful evangelist threw himself wholeheartedly into the work. At first he traveled alone, from town to town and from village to village. He walked thousands of miles. When his clothes wore out he patched them. He knew what it was to go for days with very little food. It mattered not whether it was summer or winter, wet or dry, hot or cold—John never stopped working.

His first trip took him through the towns and hamlets of Maine. Like Joseph Bates, he ranged far and wide. Then he made a long trip through Maine, New Hampshire, Vermont, and Canada West, as the province of Ontario was then called. With him went that dauntless pioneer Joseph Bates, the first of the Advent leaders to accept the seventh-day Sabbath.

On their trip through Canada, Andrews and his companion trudged for miles through deep snow. Sometimes they were able to find stage coaches going where they wanted to go. They visited large cities, traveling by train from one to another.

When Andrews learned of the many new States being organized in the West he determined to visit them. Realizing that two workers could do more than one, he contacted Hiram Edson, a farmer in western New York who had turned preacher. Edson listened to John's request, and agreed to go with him. Andrews was thin and suffered from a bad cough. Edson warned him against working so hard.

"Brother John," he protested, "you are going to shorten your life. You must slow down and get more rest."

"I can't do it," replied Andrews. "I feel as did the apostle Paul, 'Woe is me if I preach not the gospel.' How can I rest when souls are perishing who do not know Christ as their Saviour?"

So the two men worked together. They were the first evangelists to win a convert to the Sabbath in the State of Pennsylvania.

"A portion of our journey," wrote Edson, "was through a country that was new. The roads were new and rough, over cradle knolls, stumps, and rough log ways, slough holes, and trees fallen across our pathway. Much of our route was through deep valleys, and deep and narrow ravines, with almost perpendicular banks, so that fallen trees reaching across the ravine from bank to bank, were many feet above our heads as we drove beneath them. Then again we were climbing the mountains and high hills of the Alleghenies."

Traveling with a horse and buggy supplied by Edson, the two men covered six hundred miles in six weeks, a great distance in those days.

A typical day saw them hitch up a horse and buggy in the morning. They took breakfast with the family that had kindly put them up for the night. Then they would drive along the rough roads in western Pennsylvania until late in the afternoon. Coming to a small community, they would look for a suitable building in which to hold a meeting.

Sometimes it was a schoolhouse, sometimes a frontier church. Having decided where they might hold the service, the two men then went from house to house inviting each family to the meeting. Usually everyone in the village came, and John would preach, using his chart with the pictures of the beasts in Daniel and Revelation. It was not easy to secure decisions. However, now and then they left new believers, to whom the *Review and Herald* would be sent.

At the close of each meeting Brother Edson would ask whether there might be someone in the village who could put them up for the night. Usually some kindhearted family would make them welcome and allow them to spread their blankets on the floor. Sometimes John would ask for a candle and permission to use the kitchen table. There he would sit hour after hour, writing articles for the *Review and Herald.*

Hiram Edson continued to protest.

"John, you are wearing yourself out. Can't you forget the paper for a time?"

John held up a small pamphlet.

"Here is an article by O. R. L. Crosier, a man who used to keep the Sabbath. Now he is trying to persuade everyone that the first day is the true Sabbath. I am writing a series of articles proving from the Bible that he is wrong."

Then John would dip his pen in the ink and go on writing. It might be two or three o'clock in the morning before he would lie down for a few hours' sleep.

Sometimes Edson heard Andrews praying for divine help.

"O Lord," he cried, "help me to smite this thing!
Help me to smite it hard!"

Month after month John mailed his articles to the
Review office. James White, the editor, read them
with delight.

"Thank God for John Andrews," he said to a
friend. "He has become our strongest champion for
God's true Sabbath!"

INTERRUPTED MISSION

JAMES WHITE published *The Review and Herald* in Paris, Maine, for about eight months. Then he moved to Saratoga Springs, New York, where he published for about the same length of time. In 1852 he moved his printing office from Saratoga Springs to Rochester, New York.

When church members were faced with perplexing questions they usually wrote to Elder White, who printed their letters in the *Review*. There was one question that came up again and again in those early days: When is the correct time to begin the Sabbath? To settle the problem, the Adventist leaders called for a conference.

"We must observe the Sabbath from sunrise to sunrise," maintained one brother. "In Matthew 28:1 it speaks of the end of the Sabbath 'as it began to dawn toward the first day of the week.' That proves that Sabbath ends at dawn. Then it must have begun at sunrise also."

Another spoke up, "The Sabbath begins and ends at midnight."

Still another declared positively that it doesn't matter just when we begin or end the Sabbath so long as we observe twenty-four hours.

"Not so," protested Elder Bates, the oldest of the Sabbathkeeping leaders. "God makes it plain in Leviticus 23:32 where it says, 'From even unto even, shall ye celebrate your sabbath.' So the Sabbath begins at even."

"But when does 'even' begin?"

"At six o'clock," answered Elder Bates.

Others insisted that the Sabbath began at sunset. It seemed impossible for the believers to agree on the subject.

"I would sooner trust Elder Bates's judgment than anybody else's," declared Elder White. "He was our first Sabbathkeeping champion."

Elder White's stand explains why for several years the Sabbathkeeping Adventists kept Sabbath from 6:00 P.M. on Friday until 6:00 P.M. on Saturday.

Still, many members were not completely satisfied. Finally, in an effort to settle the question, James White invited Elder Andrews to study the problem further. As a result, John wrote an article for the *Review* that proved from the Bible that the evening began at sunset. For him the verse found in Mark 1:32 was conclusive: "At even, when the sun did set."

Thus the question was finally settled. Sabbath was from sunset to sunset. Because of experiences like this, John Andrews became recognized as the leading Bible scholar among the Adventists.

The young preacher continued his public work. Traveling north, south, east, and west, he visited scores of towns and hamlets.

In September, 1852, Elder White invited all Sabbathkeepers to attend a conference in Rochester. John Andrews regarded this as an opportunity to hold a series of evangelistic meetings in the city. So powerful were his sermons and so clear his arguments that all over Rochester people were talking about the 23-year-old preacher.

In the city was a young Methodist lay preacher, John Loughborough, who had two or three small companies to which he ministered on Sundays. During the week he carried on his business as a salesman for patent sash locks. One day a Methodist deacon visited Loughborough's shop and asked him a question.

"Elder Loughborough, don't you think you should go and hear the Advent preacher?"

Loughborough shook his head.

"I am not going near him. It keeps me busy studying truth. I have no time left for listening to heresy."

"Well, some of your members are going there, and you are in danger of losing them. What kind of shepherd are you to let the flock be enticed like that?"

Loughborough hadn't thought about that. For a moment he had nothing to say. The man went on. "Why don't you go down tonight and take some key Bible texts proving we aren't under the law anymore. When the Advent preacher invites questions, you just get up and let him have it. It won't take you long to demolish his arguments."

"I'll do that very thing," replied Loughborough decisively. "Thanks for telling me."

So that evening, armed with a number of Bible texts that he felt sure would quickly overthrow John Andrews' arguments, he went to the meeting. The visiting preacher talked about the change of the Sabbath. And he used the very texts Loughborough had expected to read to prove that Sunday was the right day to keep.

Andrews proved that the seventh-day Sabbath was never abolished. When he had finished he invited questions. Poor John Loughborough had nothing to say. All his arguments had already been answered and overthrown.

From that night on, Loughborough went to every meeting. When they closed, three weeks later, he was among those baptized. For the rest of his life John Loughborough looked upon John Andrews as his spiritual father, although he was only three years younger than the evangelist. In John Loughborough, Andrews had won a man who would devote seventy years to proclaiming the Advent message in many parts of the world.

There was no organized Seventh-day Adventist Church in those days. So, when James White needed a hand press to use in printing the *Review and Herald*, he bought it himself. This made him its owner. Soon some jealous, suspicious people began to whisper that Elder White was getting rich by selling his papers. When Elder White heard of these rumors he was sick at heart. Actually, he was in debt.

In order to dispel these reports, a publishing committee consisting of Elders R. F. Cottrell, John Andrews, and Uriah Smith made a study into the finances of the printing work. Through the *Review* they reported to the church that the charges were false.

Meanwhile, John Andrews continued his preaching and writing. For five years nearly every number of the *Review* contained an article written by him. It is hard to know just when he did all this writing, for he was traveling by day and preaching by night. Sometimes he spoke twelve to fifteen times in a single week. Is it any wonder that he was to have continual trouble with his voice, or that he was often too hoarse to preach?

One thing gave Elder Andrews sadness of heart: some of the very men who had once preached the Sabbath turned their backs on it and began to attack the truth.

Among them were such prominent preachers as O. R. L. Crosier, J. B. Cook, and T. M. Preble. It was, it will be remembered, Preble's first tract that had con-

vinced Andrews that he should keep the Bible Sabbath.
Sadly he wrote to two of his former companions, "I
have loved you both for the testimony you once bore to
the truth of God. My heart has bled to witness your
strange course since. But I leave you to the mercy of
God whose commandments you dare to fight."

During a meeting at New Haven, Vermont, not far
from William Miller's old home, John N. Andrews and
two other ministers were ordained. This solemn cere-
mony was carried out by two visiting ministers, Elders
James White and Joseph Baker. From then on, John was
a full-fledged minister.

John continued his evangelistic work, going from
State to State and at the same time writing for the *Review
and Herald*. During the five-year period of his most intense labor he wrote articles containing some 170,000
words. He had not yet adopted the principles of health
reform, which included rest and relaxation, for that particular light was not emphasized in the church until
1863.

It is not surprising that finally his health broke
down completely. From long hours spent poring over
books, his eyes were severely damaged. At the same
time, his voice gave out, making further public ministry impossible.

Consequently, he turned his steps toward Rochester, intending to counsel with Elder White before
returning to his father's farm, where he hoped to regain his shattered health.

One cold February day James White glanced out
of the window of his house on Hope Avenue and saw
a stoop-shouldered man turning in at the gate. He was
leaning on a cane, and walking slowly. Something
about the figure seemed strangely familiar. Elder
White stepped out onto the veranda to greet the visitor. He hoped the man was not a beggar, for there was

little food in the house.

"Is there something I can do for you?" asked James White.

The man stopped, then looked up.

"Is it possible, Elder White, that you don't recognize me?"

The voice was weak, but Elder White knew immediately who his visitor was.

"Elder Andrews! Is it really you?"

"Yes, Elder White. At least it is all that is left of me."

"What have you been doing to yourself?" He took John's hand in his and shook it warmly. "You look as if you have lost your last friend."

"My health is gone, and I am completely discouraged. I can no longer labor in the Lord's vineyard."

James White led John Andrews into the house, where they talked for a long time. John described his strenuous experiences. It was no wonder he had had a breakdown in health.

Elder White listened patiently, then said kindly, "What are you planning to do, John? Why not stay with us for a while until you get to feeling better? We have a room for you. I'll even give you a desk on which to write. I don't know what we would have done during the past five years without your wonderful articles."

"No, Brother White, I can't stay with you long. I must return to my father's farm. Perhaps outdoor work on the land will help restore my health. Besides, my father really needs me."

But John Andrews did join the White family in the Rochester printing office for about ten weeks. He was happy to find there his friend and son in the gospel, John Loughborough. Uriah Smith was also there, but Uriah's sister, Annie, stricken with tuberculosis, had returned to her home, where she was to die.

Annie would never be forgotten. During her stay at Rochester she had written a number of poems, some of which were later set to music. We still sing a number of her hymns, such as "How Far From Home?" and "Blessed Jesus, Meek and Lowly." But of all her hymns, the one best remembered is "I Saw One Weary." It is Number 371 in our *Church Hymnal*. The first stanza describes Joseph Bates, and the second James White.

The third stanza applies best to John Andrews:

"And there was one who left behind
The treasured friends of early years,
And honor, pleasure, wealth resigned,
To tread the path bedewed with tears.
Through trials deep and conflicts sore,
Yet still a smile of joy he wore;
I asked what buoyed his spirits up,
'O this!' said he—'the blessed hope.' "

The little group at Rochester offered many earnest prayers for Elder Andrews, and there was some improvement in his health. But because the weakness of his eyes would not permit him to read or write, he decided there was little he could do in Rochester. He therefore carried out his original plan and returned to Paris, where he spent the summer of 1855 with his parents. When he said good-by to his Rochester friends, James White placed twenty-five dollars in his hands and bade him Godspeed.

Elder White's concern for John Andrews led him to make a pathetic appeal on his behalf in the next issue of the *Review and Herald*. To the church members far and near, many of whom were Elder Andrews' converts, James White wrote:

"But few persons have any idea of his sacrifices,

and present discouragements. . . . He has toiled on, day and night, with little regard for health. . . . He is penniless and feeble. . . . His father is one of the poor of this world, and quite infirm, and his only brother a cripple. Judge of our feelings to see a dear brother, a fellow laborer, with whom we have toiled side by side for years, placed in this situation. . . . He has toiled so incessantly for your salvation that he is broken down at the age of twenty-five."

Elder White then invited those who were able, to send contributions to Rochester on behalf of Elder Andrews.

When John received the *Review and Herald* containing Elder White's suggestion, he was surprised and considerably embarrassed. Always a very humble man, he wrote that the appeal had caused him "much pain." At the same time he thanked those who had responded and added, "I wish to say in conclusion that I did not return home to leave the work of God. The promotion of the cause of truth is still the great object of my life."

Did John Andrews think back to the day when his Uncle Charles had offered to pay all expenses connected with his attending any university in the land? If he did, the recollection brought him no regrets. He had set his hand to the plow, and for him there was no turning back. If God would give him back his health and strength he would again take up the work he loved so much.

ACROSS
the
MISSISSIPPI

IT WAS on a chilly morning in early spring that John Andrews alighted from the stagecoach in Paris, Maine. Walking along the street toward his father's farm, he met several friends and neighbors. Although he recognized them, John appeared a complete stranger to them. Who could recognize in this rather seedy-looking person the tall, dignified scholar who had left home several years before to preach the Advent message?

When he arrived at his home he was greeted joyfully by his father and mother. As Sarah Andrews threw her arms around her son, she exclaimed, "John, John, whatever have you done to yourself? You are skin and bones!" A faithful reader of the *Review and Herald,* Edward Andrews had traced his son's travels from place to place in its columns. However, nothing that John had written prepared his parents for the arrival of this broken-down young man, worn out at the age of 26.

It was a long story that John told his parents as they sat around the blazing fire that evening. When he finished, his father asked, "What are your plans for the future?"

"First of all I must regain my health. Without that, there is simply no future for me. Spring will soon be here, and with it plenty of work. I'll be glad to help you on the farm. Working in the open air will help me more than anything else."

Sarah Andrews laid her hand on her son's arm as she asked him a very serious question.

"John, you are 26 and still single. Do you mean to tell me that in all your travels you haven't found a girl you might want for a wife?"

"To tell the truth, Mother," John replied, "I really haven't had time to think of marriage. It would have been cruel to drag a wife around to all the places I have visited. Could I in all fairness ask any woman to endure the hardships that have broken me down so completely?"

"Then you don't intend to marry?" his father asked.

"I didn't say that. But if I do want a wife, I don't think I need to look any farther than to the girls right here in Paris."

"You're perfectly right, John," his mother responded. "I'm not the one to give you advice about such matters. But I tell you this much: there is one girl in Paris who, whenever I see her, asks whether I have had any word from you."

"Now I am the one to be curious," replied John with a smile. "It couldn't be Angeline Stevens, could it, Mother?"

"I wasn't going to tell you, but since you have guessed it, yes, she is the one."

"I know she likes me, and I'm very fond of her. Perhaps a friendship will develop this summer. I must go and see her tomorrow. You know she is five years older than I, but that really doesn't make much difference."

John and his parents talked far into the night. Father has certainly aged fast since I left home, John thought to himself. He is going to need more and more help, especially since William can't be of much assistance.

The next day John called on Angeline Stevens. She was as shocked by his appearance as his parents had been. She could see that whoever married him would have a hard time keeping him out of an early grave. These thoughts, however, she kept strictly to herself. Their visit was pleasant and enjoyable to both.

The sun returned from the Southland, and spring merged into summer. With the return of warm weather, plenty of exercise, and pleasant surroundings, John's health improved steadily. But because he was plagued by a chronic sinus condition, he was in no condition to go preaching again. For many years this health problem was to plague him and make his life miserable.

For the returned son, the best in the house was provided. John had always loved his mother's cooking, and was now tempted to eat far too much for his own good, particularly of sweets.

One day in June the mailman brought a copy of the *Review and Herald* that was to change the course of the Andrewses' lives. Not only would the Andrews family be affected by this article but other Adventists in Paris also.

As John glanced through the paper, looking for reports of what his friends and former companions were doing, he came across a short article primarily addressed to the believers in New England.

"Why not move west, brethren?" it asked. "The soil is rich and deep and easy to work. You will find it very different from the rocky hillsides you have cultivated for years. The harvest field is wide open to you and the people will listen to our message. The work needed to win one convert in the East will bring in twenty in the West."

The next time the family were all together John Andrews picked up the *Review* and read the article to them. He knew something of the fertile West.

"Everything the paper says is absolutely right, Father. Why stay here, wearing yourself out on these stony fields, when all that rich black soil is just waiting for someone to cultivate it? Let's sell out and go West. Thousands of others are doing it every year. Then, if God gives me strength, I'll use it for Him in those new western States."

Edward Andrews made no reply. But he thought about what John had said during the days that followed. It would not be easy to pull up roots and transplant his family to a faraway place. He had lived all his life in Maine. Here his ancestors had lived and died.

But John's enthusiasm and determination won the day. That summer the family made steady preparations for the move. Their enthusiasm spread among their neighbors, and a few families agreed to go with them. However, Angeline's family decided to remain in Paris for the time being. This was a great disappointment to John.

The animals were sold, and the crops were disposed of. Then, with their household goods, they set out to make a new home in the West. Their journey took them across New Hampshire, down through Vermont, and into New York to Rochester on the Erie Canal.

At Rochester John was happy to meet his friend John Loughborough again. But he was sorry to learn that Loughborough had been having a hard time. Four days each week he worked on farms around

Rochester, receiving one dollar per day. Over week-
ends he preached in Adventist churches and country
schoolhouses. He would not know until the end of
the summer, when the committee would meet, how
much he would be paid for his church work.

Andrews tried to persuade his friend to accompany
him to Iowa. Loughborough shook his head.

"Not now. Perhaps sometime later. I doubt
whether I have enough cash to get my family across
the State line. I'll have to wait and see how it goes."

John found Elder and Mrs. White and their staff
still in the Rochester office. They were not going to
be there long, for they were preparing to move to
Battle Creek, Michigan. Elder White was happy to see
John Andrews and commented on his improved appearance. He was pleased to learn of the party's intended destination.

"It's a fruitful land, John," he told Andrews. "Everything grows in Iowa, they say. What pleases me is
to see our church membership growing in those western States. By the way, you haven't written much for
the *Review* this year. I hope your silence is only tem-
porary."

"You'll hear from me again, once we are settled in
Iowa," promised the writer.

The Andrews family pushed on westward. It was
November before they arrived at their destination and
moved onto their farm near the small town of Waukon.

Everything they had heard about Iowa proved
true. The topsoil was incredibly rich, and once the
tough prairie grass had been uprooted, was easy to
work.

"You couldn't build a stone wall here if you
wanted one," John wrote to Angeline. He went on to
urge that the Stevens family come and join the other
Adventists living in and around Waukon.

It was a race against time to get houses built before the cold and heavy snows of winter arrived. They
had thought New England winters were severe, but
those in Iowa seemed even worse. During those
months John clerked in a store owned and operated
by relatives.

Somehow the settlers survived that first winter,
and in the spring they planted large fields of grain.
That summer brought new recruits to the Adventist
colony. The family of Cyprian Stevens arrived and
took up a claim near that of Edward Andrews. Naturally, John was delighted to have Angeline near, and
he visited with her whenever he could find the time in
his busy program. Out of these visits came their decision to be married in the autumn, as soon as the
harvest was gathered in.

John was happy when his eyesight improved
enough so he could read for ever-lengthening periods
of time. As he followed the ox-drawn plow, he carried
a Greek or Hebrew Bible in his pocket. Whenever the
oxen stopped to rest he would take out his Bible and
learn a few new phrases in one of those languages.

The arrival of John Loughborough with his family
cheered the heart of John Andrews. The two men
talked over prospects for the future. Andrews urged
Loughborough to take up a claim and put in a crop,
pointing out that if he did he would find himself a
prosperous farmer by the end of two or three seasons.

"By the way," John asked one day, "how much did
the committee pay you for your summer's work?"

"Well, it averaged four dollars per week," Loughborough answered.

"Was that all!"

"Yes, that was all. I told my wife we simply
couldn't go on as we had been living. So we did odd
jobs during the winter, saved our money, bought a

team, and came here. From the looks of things a man
would have to be a pretty poor farmer not to make
money here. Besides, I can always fall back on my
trade as a carpenter. Buildings are going up in all
directions, and carpenters are in great demand."

"That's right," agreed Andrews. "I intend to take
up a land claim for myself as soon as Angeline and
I are married."

Although from a material standpoint the future
looked bright for the Adventists living in and around
Waukon, their spiritual condition was languishing.
Seeing prosperity apparently within their grasp, they
concentrated all their energy on growing more and
more corn, and raising increasingly large herds of
cattle.

To their way of thinking, the future looked bright.
They added more land to their holdings. They worked
from fourteen to eighteen hours a day, often until
dark, even on Fridays, apparently indifferent to the
fact that they were breaking the Sabbath. As their
own money in the bank increased, their donations to
the church declined. There was little time for missionary work, or to be the light God intended they should
be.

Even John Andrews was influenced by the growing tide of indifference. The articles he had promised
to write for the *Review* were forgotten. No wonder
James White wrote in the church paper, "Why don't
the brethren who used to write, and others who can,
write for the *Review and Herald?* Where are brethren
Pierce and Andrews? The inquiry goes around in the
church, 'Why don't THEY write?' "

Mrs. White was deeply troubled. The condition of
the church members in Waukon was shown to her in
vision. Souls were in danger of being lost. The bright
light that had been kindled in Iowa was in danger of

going out in darkness. If the services of John Andrews and J. N. Loughborough were lost to God's work it would be very serious indeed.

A meeting was called for workers and believers at Round Grove, Illinois. The Whites were there, and a revival took place.

"We must go to Waukon now," said Ellen White firmly when the workers' meeting had ended.

Her husband looked at her in astonishment.

"How are we going to get to Waukon in the middle of winter?" he asked. "It's two hundred miles from here."

"We must go," Mrs. White repeated.

Two of the workers offered to drive the Whites there in their open sleigh. Just as they were ready to start, it began to rain. It looked as if the snow would soon turn to slush over the sticky mud. If that happened, how could they travel?

"We'll have to call off the trip," James told his wife.

"Sister White, what about Waukon?" asked one of the men who had volunteered to take them.

"We shall go," she replied.

"All right, we'll go," he agreed, "but the Lord will have to work a miracle to make it possible."

During the following night, James White couldn't sleep. All night long, he and Mrs. White kept getting up and looking out of the window at the rain pouring down. They continued to pray for snow, and their prayer was answered. Shortly before dawn the temperature dropped and the rain changed to snow. All day it fell, and soon there was plenty for sleighing. The group set out at dawn the next day and glided across Illinois, toward Iowa. Then another problem arose. They found there was too much snow! At one place they were held up for a full week by a snowstorm. Finally it cleared, and they rode on.

They came to the banks of the broad Mississippi. The river was frozen from bank to bank, but the ice was thin. The manager of the hotel at which they stopped warned them that it would be dangerous to try to cross. That night it rained again, depositing more water on the already weakened ice. The water on the ice was now nearly a foot deep.

People living along the river heard that a party of travelers was planning to cross the river on the ice. The next morning they gathered to see what those rash travelers would do.

"This rain will make the ice rotten," they warned. "You'll never get across. Others have tried it and broken through."

"What now, Ellen?" asked James White.

"We shall go to Waukon," was her firm reply.

the LONG ROAD BACK

WHEN THE time came to cross the river the rain was still falling. The driver turned to Elder and Mrs. White and put the question bluntly.

"Is it on to Iowa, or back to Illinois? We have come to the Red Sea. Shall we cross?"

Ellen White's answer came with assurance. "Go forward, trusting in Israel's God." Elder White agreed.

Slowly they drove down the bank and onto the ice, then headed for the far shore. The horses splashed through the water; the ice made a cracking sound as they passed over it. Word had spread, and people on both sides of the river had rushed to the banks expecting to see horses, sleigh, and passengers disappear beneath the ice.

After what seemed like a long time, the sleigh reached the Iowa shore. As it finally drew up on the bank the passengers burst into a song of praise. One of the watchers greeted the party with the words, "I wouldn't cross that river with horse and sleigh for a thousand dollars."

Since it was Friday, the travelers drove to the nearest town and found hotel rooms for the Sabbath.

Sunday morning they started on the last lap of their journey. The rain had stopped, but an icy wind blew out of the north, chilling the passengers to the bone. But they pushed on, stopping at hotels for warm food and shelter, reaching Waukon on Wednesday. When the group of Sabbathkeepers heard that the Whites had arrived they could hardly believe it. Some of them were not happy; they had lost touch with God.

"You must stay with us," said Edward Andrews to Elder and Mrs. White. The other visitors went to the Stevens home. It did John Andrews' heart good to be close again to the warm, dynamic James White.

"We have come to hold some meetings," Elder White announced.

Meetings! It had been a long time since the Waukon company had enjoyed real Christian fellowship. In the meetings that followed, Ellen White pointed out the cold condition of the Waukon believers. During one meeting she was given a vision and shown more about the conditions in the church. A revival took place. Prayers, songs, and confessions arose to God. Wrongs were made right.

John Andrews was deeply touched by the messages. He promised that as soon as he had regained his health he would return to the Lord's work. He also told James White he would resume writing for the *Review and Herald.*

John Loughborough had left the work because of discouragement. Now he realized that his faith had been too weak. Standing in the midst of the Waukon Adventists, he declared, "I have put away my hammer. I have driven my last nail as a public carpenter. Henceforth my hand shall hold the sword of the Spirit, and never give it up. So help me, God!"

For Loughborough there was no more turning

back. He returned with the Whites to Illinois and began working among the churches.

Angeline Stevens made a good wife for John. Being married to an Adventist minister in those days meant weeks and sometimes months of separation, but Angeline accepted the situation and made no attempt to hold John back when duty called.

As John's health returned he took a more active part in the work of the church. Occasionally he would travel to Battle Creek for a conference with the leaders. They could see that physically he was still in no condition to return to his former manner of work, but he kept his promise and wrote regularly for the *Review.*

One afternoon as John was working in the cornfield he looked up to see Angeline running toward him. Her flushed face and evident distress convinced him that something serious had happened. He hurried to meet her.

Panting for breath, she managed to gasp out her message.

"Oh, John, do come quick. Pa's been bitten bad by a rattlesnake."

John ran to the Stevens home. He found his friend and father-in-law lying on a bed, evidently in shock. Mrs. Stevens had wrapped a cloth tightly around his arm above the bite. John examined the wound and noted the deep puncture marks made by the snake's fangs. A local doctor was called. He recommended brandy, but otherwise had no practical suggestions to offer. Mr. Stevens' sufferings were intense.

"O Father," he cried out more than once, "give sustaining grace!" On the fifth day he lost the battle. He was laid to rest in the local cemetery.

During those early years James White was struggling with the problem of how Adventist workers could be fairly paid. In some communities they were well supported by the church members. In other places the members were less generous. In areas where there were no Adventists the preachers found it very difficult to support themselves and their families.

Workers were expected to be largely self-supporting, laboring at various trades or helping farmers during the week and preaching on Sabbaths. Elder White felt that the church would make faster progress if ministers were paid regular salaries. How was it done in Bible times? he wondered.

If anyone could find the answer it would be John Andrews, the foremost scholar in the church. Elder White called for a meeting of all the nearby ministers. A special invitation was extended to John Andrews to be present. Responding to the invitation, he went to the meeting and helped launch a plan called systematic benevolence. It was based on the principle that every member should pay according to what he earns.

While the meeting was in progress Ellen White became very sick. John Andrews was one of those who prayed for her recovery. God heard, and restored her to health.

Gradually John began to travel again. James White reported in the *Review* that Brother J. N. Andrews, of Iowa, had visited the Battle Creek church and spoken twice. It was, in Elder White's words, "a spiritual feast." And John was present at the meeting in Battle Creek in 1860 when the name Seventh-day Adventist was chosen for the church.

The outbreak of the Civil War the following year brought deep trouble to everyone, including Adventists.

This was the first war involving the United States

after the founding of the Seventh-day Adventist Church, and it caused many problems. At first all of the soldiers were volunteers, and Adventists did not need to sign up. But, as the war dragged on, there were continual calls for more and more soldiers. Strong pressure was put on every able-bodied man to induce him to go into the armed forces.

Many letters came to the *Review and Herald,* asking whether Seventh-day Adventists could fight. How could they shoulder guns and shoot someone else without breaking the sixth commandment, "Thou shalt not kill." The obvious answer was that they could not. When the time came and draft boards were set up to force men into the Army, the troubles of Adventists increased.

James White gave the matter much study. Would it not be possible, he wondered, to have the Adventist Church identified as being opposed to taking life? Could they be recognized as noncombatants, like the Quakers? John Andrews was asked to collect necessary information and lay the matter before the officers in President Lincoln's Government.

One day as Andrews was busy working on this project a friend, Mr. Kinne, called. In his hand Kinne carried a notice indicating that he had been selected by the draft board to serve in the Federal Army, and ordering him to present himself to a doctor for a physical examination.

"Would you be willing to go with me?" Kinne asked Andrews.

"Of course. I don't think there is much danger of their accepting you. You are too thin and not rugged enough to stand army life."

The two men went to the doctor's office. Andrews remained outside, praying that his friend would be rejected. But, contrary to his hopes, Kinne was accepted and told to report for induction.

It was a sober-faced Kinne who informed John that he had been accepted.

"My poor wife and children! What will happen to them? I have a feeling that I will never return if I go into the Army."

Andrews keenly felt the sorrow of his friend. There was only one way to save him from the Army. The Government was willing to exempt him if he paid $300 to the provost marshal. This money would be used to hire some other man to go in his place. Elder Andrews quietly told some of his friends of Kinne's trouble. Among themselves they raised $300 and so saved Brother Kinne.

Three years later, when Mrs. Andrews had to go to the Danville Sanitarium for long and expensive treatment, Andrews wrote his friend Kinne asking for the loan of some money. Kinne was pleased that his friend should turn to him in his perplexity.

"I see the hand of the Lord in this," exclaimed Kinne. The very day he had received John's letter, he had balanced his books and found he had a profit of $1,300. It gave him great pleasure to send a generous loan to which he attached a cash gift of forty dollars.

"You cast your bread on the waters when you helped me stay out of the Army," wrote Kinne, "and now part of it is coming back to you."

To prepare the way for his visit to Washington, Andrews wrote to the governors of some States where many Adventists lived, asking whether they would accept Adventists as noncombatants and permit them to work along life-saving lines. They replied they would be happy to do so.

Armed with these documents, Andrews went to Washington. He spent several weeks talking with various officials in the Lincoln administration. Before he left, the problem had been solved. He returned to Battle Creek to report that from then on Adventists would not be required to bear arms.

The home of John and Angeline was a happy one. John became the proud father of a son, born in 1857, and of a daughter, born four years later. These children, Charles and Mary, brought much comfort to Angeline while father was away on his evangelistic tours.

Naturally, John longed to be at home so that he might enjoy his family. He felt that his children needed him. But he had become one of the most powerful preachers in the Adventist Church, and calls requesting his services were coming from many churches and conferences. Because Rochester, New York, was central for his travels, it became his headquarters. However, Angeline and the children remained in Waukon.

In 1864 the officers of the New York Conference suggested to James White that a subscription list be started by the *Review* for those willing to help buy a house for the Andrews family, so they might be together more often. Elder White thought it was a good idea.

However, before promoting the project, Elder White pointed out that it would not be right to try to keep Elder Andrews continually in New York State. He went on to say, "When New York can spare him, New England may deserve and demand his services for a while. Brother Andrews is not the property of any one State, but is God's servant to work here and there. . . . So send in your pledges, brethren." James and Ellen White started the list off with a gift.

The necessary money was raised. A house was bought at 313 Main Street in Rochester and handed over to Elder Andrews. Deeply embarrassed that such a collection should be made, he nevertheless graciously accepted the gift as a sign of the love and esteem of his fellow believers, and wrote a thank-you letter, which appeared in the *Review and Herald*. When all the arrangements were complete he went to Iowa, packed his belongings, and moved his family to Rochester. For the next eight years their home was to be in Rochester.

By this time John Andrews was one of the most eloquent preachers in the denomination. With the "gospel tent" he and his companion, an Elder Fuller, went from place to place, holding meetings nearly every night. Farmers came in their wagons and townspeople in their buggies. At the close of each series of meetings, ten, twenty, thirty, or more persons were usually baptized, another church was organized, and the tent would move on. Sometimes as many as four such efforts would be held by them in a single summer.

While John was laboring in Maine, Father Andrews took to his bed for the last time, sick with tuberculosis. His wife, Sarah, asked whether they should telegraph John to return home.

Father Andrews shook his head.

"There is nothing he can do for me. Tell him I die in the faith, and will meet him when Jesus comes."

On April 14, 1865, Edward Andrews fell asleep at the age of 67.

HEALTHFUL LIVING

ANGELINE ANDREWS was worried. Something was wrong with the right leg of her 2-year-old son, Charles. For several days she had watched him carefully. Now she was certain he was limping.

I wonder if he fell and hurt himself? I'll ask Mother Andrews what I should do, she decided. The next time Angeline visited her mother-in-law, Charles went with her.

"I want you to look at Charles when he walks," she whispered to Sarah.

Mrs. Andrews took her place on the opposite side of the room from her daughter-in-law and grandson. She held out two cookies to the boy.

"Come, Charles, here's a cooky for you."

Charles walked over and took it. "Now take this one to your mother." She placed the second cooky in his hands, then watched as he limped back to Angeline.

Charles was sent out to play while two very concerned women discussed the problem. Both were convinced that the lad did indeed walk with a limp.

"I don't think you should worry too much about it," said Mother Andrews. "He may have hurt it somehow. Most childhood problems disappear if given time."

Angeline tried not to worry. When her husband returned to Waukon from his next trip she talked with him about Charles and his limp, which was becoming more noticeable every day. They decided to take the child to see a doctor. The man examined the foot; he twisted it in various directions. It didn't seem to pain Charles. The doctor shook his head.

"I really don't know what's wrong with the foot," he said. "I don't think surgery would help, at least not yet." Sadly the parents took their child home.

During the next four years Charles's parents watched as the condition of his right foot became steadily worse. By the time he was 6, in 1863, it had turned at right angles to his leg, and the entire limb was very thin, although it was the same length as the normal leg. By this time Charles could only hobble. In the night he often cried out in his sleep from the pain. No doctor held out any hope of a cure.

John Andrews would kneel by the bedside of his son and offer up fervent prayers for him. Would he be a cripple all his life? Or would that life be shortened by some mysterious disease?

In 1863 Ellen White was given a vision concerning healthful living. The changes in daily life called for in that vision were so revolutionary that some Adventists simply didn't try to carry them out. But the Andrews family decided to make a start. Face to face with tragedy, John and Angeline determined to accept and follow the light given.

Their first change was in the method of treatment they were using on Charles. They began using hot-and-cold fomentations on the crippled leg. These treatments gave quick relief. The change in the little patient's condition seemed miraculous. Gradually the foot assumed normal position and size.

John and Angeline Andrews did some serious thinking. If one phase of health reform could do so much for their son, what might they not expect for their family if they should adopt the whole program? They decided to follow the instructions given.

Away went spices, pepper, vinegar, butter, meat, fish, and heavy meals. They baked their bread from whole-wheat flour. They cut down on the use of salt, and ate only two meals a day. When possible, they ate an abundance of fruits and fresh vegetables. In those days, before refrigeration, the problem of finding fruit and vegetables in winter was a serious one.

This new program brought quick relief from the many ills that had plagued John Andrews for so many years. No longer did he waken in the morning feeling as if two wildcats were fighting in his stomach. There were no more big doses of pills and medicines. His dyspepsia disappeared. For the first time since his boyhood days in Paris, he really enjoyed good health. He wrote to Elder White at the *Review* office describing his program and the resulting progress toward better health. He regarded health reform as the prime cause.

There was one aspect of health reform, however, to which he paid scant attention. He was not temperate in his working hours. Not only did his day begin before daylight but he frequently worked in his office at night until eleven or twelve o'clock, or even till one o'clock in the morning. By so doing he wore out his body; later he was to pay a high price for this form of intemperance.

In 1865 James White was elected president of the General Conference. A few months later, he was stricken with paralysis. He was not the only worker in Battle Creek who suffered a breakdown in health during that sad spring and summer. On September 14 Elder and Mrs. White, John Loughborough, and Uriah Smith all left by what was known as the "invalids' " train for the water-cure treatment at Dansville, New York.

Dr. Jackson, the head of the institution, carefully looked over the group of Adventist patients. After examining Elder White he was not optimistic. Mr. White, he insisted, should remain at the "Home on the Hillside" for six or eight months. Elder Loughborough, he thought, needed five or six months of complete rest. Elder Smith might be cured within five or six weeks.

At the time, John Andrews was working among the churches in Maine. He was known as a mighty man of prayer, and James White, who thought very highly of Elder Andrews and had a great deal of faith in his prayers, begged that he be sent for. The word was relayed, and John set out. But before he could reach the stricken General Conference president, Ellen White had moved her husband from Dansville to Rochester. Here she found a place for him to live at the home of a Brother Lamson for several weeks. And there Elder Andrews found him. With other ministers he prayed, and they anointed Elder White.

Those prayers were answered. James White began to recover, and by the first of January he was strong enough to return to Battle Creek. But he was still far from being well. He did not feel strong enough to attend the General Conference session held in May, 1866. It was an act of faith on the part of the brethren when they re-elected him president, and on his part when he accepted.

The sickness of their leaders made Adventists realize that health was precious. To spread the principles of health reform among the Adventists, Mrs. White had, in 1865, prepared a series of articles on the general subject "How to Live." Now this instruction was carefully read by the church members.

While the Whites were in Rochester Mrs. White had a vision that brought far-reaching changes in the Adventist Church. The church was urged to establish an institution where the sick might be treated without the use of poisonous drugs.

It was decided that this call should be heeded. Elders Andrews and Loughborough were sent out to visit the churches to raise the money necessary to establish such an institution. They took pledges, and by May, 1866, some $11,000 had been promised. This was the beginning of medical missionary work among Seventh-day Adventists.

The new medical institution, established at Battle Creek, was known at first as the Western Health Reform Institute. A few years later the name was changed, and, as the Battle Creek Sanitarium, it became famous all over the world.

It was on the fifth of September, 1866, that the Western Health Reform Institute opened its doors to admit one patient. Thousands more were to follow.

According to Dr. Jackson, of the Dansville institution, salt was a poison and injurious to the body. Mrs. White did not accept this teaching, for the Lord had shown her that the body needs some salt.

One morning James and Ellen White and John Andrews sat down to breakfast in the Reform Institute. The principal item on the menu was a thick porridge, or mush, as it was called. It was made of whole-wheat flour, boiled in water without salt. As they began eating, John Andrews put a little milk on his porridge while James White scattered some sugar over his. Mrs. White sprinkled some salt on her porridge.

Elder Andrews spoke up in solemn tones (and he could be very solemn), "Sister White, don't you know that salt is a mineral substance and should never enter the human stomach?"

Ellen White answered simply, "Brother Andrews, my Bible says that salt is good." So far as she was concerned, that settled the matter.

In the spring of 1871 Adventists in Michigan gathered in Battle Creek for a great health-reform rally. The place where the rally was held was full to overflowing. In the afternoon there was a testimony meeting. Lay people and ministers went forward one by one and told what health reform had done for them.

Someone thought of Joseph Bates, the first health reformer in the denomination.

"Where is Elder Bates?" he called out. "We must hear Elder Bates on this subject."

Always a very modest man, the 79-year-old Joseph Bates had been sitting in a back row. In response to the call he rose, walked down the aisle, and mounted the platform. Those who saw him that day said that he "tripped along as lightly as a boy," and "stood as straight as a marble shaft."

He told how through the years he had dropped one bad habit after another until he had reached the point of total abstinence from everything harmful. In closing he said he was entirely free from aches and pains and entertained the joyful hope that if he continued on in the upward way he would, one day soon, stand without fault before the throne of God. The audience was electrified. For a few moments, only fervent Amens could be heard from all parts of the congregation.

The next speaker was John N. Andrews. Poor man, his adoption of healthful living had been far more recent than that of Elder Bates. There were smiles on all sides when Elder Andrews began to speak by quoting the words of Solomon, "What can the man do that cometh after the king?" (Eccl. 2:12).

Elder Andrews gave a convincing tribute to health reform and described how he had been saved an immense amount of suffering by adopting it. His health at this time, he said, was better than it had been when he was twenty years younger.

God was preparing His people to face the challenge of warning the world. He would need a strong people to accomplish this task. Health reform was one of His appointed means for securing such a people.

MINISTERING to the CHURCHES

IN THE summer of 1862 Elder Andrews and an Elder Newton decided to hold meetings in Adam's Center, New York. As they were pitching the conference tent they were distressed to find it full of holes.

"Brother Andrews," asked Elder Newton anxiously, "whatever can we do with our congregation when it rains?"

"We will just have to pitch it near a church building into which we can take our congregation to keep them dry," John replied.

So they pitched their tent near a Seventh Day Baptist church. After six weeks of meetings, fifty people accepted the truths taught by the evangelists. Following this the two ministers moved the tent to Fairport, a town near Rochester. There, as in other places, they found the people too excited by the events of the Civil War then raging to listen to their message.

Two years later Elder Andrews and Elder John Byington, president of the General Conference, traveled through Michigan, holding meetings in Monterey and Fair Plains.

After the trip to Rochester in the winter of 1865 to join in prayer for Elder White, described in the previous chapter, John Andrews returned to New England. Although he found the people in the western States more willing to listen and quicker to accept the message than those in New England, he still had a strong desire to carry the truth to the eastern States.

In the spring of 1866 Elder Andrews pitched his tent on a piece of land in the town of Norridgewock, Maine. To provide seats for the people, he purchased a supply of planks, which he nailed together into benches. When everything was ready he visited every house in town, inviting the people to his meetings.

At first only a few people attended. But as word spread that the dignified minister in the tent was a son of New England, the attendance increased rapidly. Never had they met anyone so well acquainted with the Bible.

John taught them things they had never heard before. The meetings lasted nearly two months. When they closed, practically every person in town went to the river and watched as sixty persons were baptized and joined the Adventist Church. To provide for the children in the group, Elder Andrews organized a Sabbath school.

During the winter, when it was impossible to hold tent meetings, Elder Andrews traveled from community to community, speaking in the churches. In the summer of 1867 he went to Washington, New Hampshire. This was one of the oldest churches in the denomination, but his heart was saddened by the cold condition of the members. One brother openly rejected the messages borne by Ellen White, and never lost an opportunity to ridicule her and her husband and cast suspicion on their work as leaders in the church. He spoke so bitterly in every meeting that the members became discouraged. For weeks there were no services of any kind—no Sabbath school, no church, and no prayer meeting.

In response to Elder Andrews' invitation, the church members gathered to hear him speak. But their attitude was so cold and hard that he felt he was making no impression whatever. Scarcely any young people came, and Andrews knew those Adventists had large families. When he met some of the youth and asked them why they didn't come to church they replied that the members were hypocrites. Elder Andrews could see that before he could help the children and youth, it would be necessary to set the adults straight. This was made difficult by the bitter brother who continued to heap abuse on Elder and Mrs. White whenever he could.

Elder Andrews next tried visiting and praying with the people in their homes, but the responses were not encouraging. He came to the home of William Farnsworth, who had stood up in the meetinghouse twenty-three years before, vowing that he would keep the Sabbath regardless of what others might do. Now William was as cold as the other church members. All of his energies were centered in taking care of his large and still-growing family. Andrews decided to make a special appeal to the young members of the Farnsworth family.

"Where are your children?" he asked William.

"Oh, here and there. Some are getting in the hay. Eugene is out in the cornfield."

John Andrews walked out past the barn, where he picked up a hoe and took it with him to the cornfield.

Eugene saw him coming and would have liked to slip away. He had no desire to talk with the preacher, but there seemed no way of escape. Elder Andrews took off his coat and hung it on the branch of a tree. He then took his place beside the youth, cultivating the rows of corn.

After they had completed several rows, Andrews suggested they rest awhile in the shade. Eugene could hardly object to that. He offered Elder Andrews a drink of water from his jug. For a few moments they sat in thought, just relaxing. Finally Elder Andrews broke the silence.

"Well, Eugene, what are you planning to make of yourself?"

"Well, Elder, first of all I intend to get an education," Eugene replied.

"Good! That will be the best thing you can do. And then what?"

"I plan to study law."

"You could do worse. And what then?"

"I intend to become the best lawyer in the State."

"And then what?"

"I hope to make a lot of money and maybe visit other countries."

"And what then?"

"I suppose I'll get married and have a nice home."

"And what then?"

"Well, I'll grow old and die like everybody else, I suppose."

Looking the young man squarely in the eye, Elder Andrews concluded with the most vital question of all.

"Eugene, what then?"

Eugene had no answer. Elder Andrews had given him something to think about. Before they parted, Andrews prayed with the young man. The seed planted that day in the heart of Eugene Farnsworth was to bear abundant fruit. Eugene did get his education. But instead of becoming a lawyer, he became a minister and guided thousands of feet to the pathway to heaven.

That fall Elder and Mrs. White toured the Eastern States, visiting many churches and holding revival

meetings. Ellen White knew all about the lukewarm
state of the church at Washington, and determined to
visit it. So word was sent ahead saying that the Whites
expected to spend part of the week before Christmas
in Washington. Elder Andrews joined the Whites
as they traveled northward by sleigh. The nearer they
came to Washington, the heavier was the snow. The
horses found it difficult to pull the sleigh through the
deep snowdrifts.

Finally they reached their destination. They were
warmly welcomed at the hospitable home of Cyrus
Farnsworth, William's younger brother. In spite of
all the church difficulties, he had retained his confidence in the message. Cyrus sent out word that there
would be a special meeting in the church. The young
people were particularly invited to come, even though
Mrs. White knew well that until the adults made
things right, confessed their sins, and repented, there
was little they could do for the youth of the church.

Worcester Ball, the man who had heaped ridicule
and abuse on Elder and Mrs. White, was there, eager
for a fight. Mrs. White had a message for him. She appealed to him to humble his heart and join his brothers and sisters in seeking God.

At first it was hard for him to do this. But God's
Spirit was present, and as Elder Andrews preached on
the sufferings of Christ and pointed out how much
Jesus had done for His followers, the preacher and
his congregation wept together.

Brother Ball's eyes were opened. He began to see
his great need. His heart was touched, and walking up
to the front of the church, he stood and begged for-
giveness. He also asked Elder and Mrs. White to for-
give him. Ministers and members shook his hand and
prayed together for him.

In the afternoon meeting, Mrs. White spoke to

various members, giving them special messages from God. Eugene Farnsworth stood near the back of the church, listening as Mrs. White pointed out the sins of the church members. He watched anxiously to see whether she would speak to his father, whom he knew was cherishing a secret sin.

William thought no one knew that he had never given up the use of tobacco. But Eugene knew. He had seen his father more than once spit out tobacco juice, then hastily push pure-white snow over the dark-brown stain. Did Mrs. White know about that? Eugene wondered. "If Sister White is a true prophet of God," he said to himself, "she will rebuke my father."

Eugene did not have to wait long. Mrs. White pointed to William Farnsworth and said, "I see that this brother is a slave to tobacco. The worst of it is that he is trying to deceive his brethren into thinking that he has stopped using it."

From that day on William Farnsworth chewed no more tobacco. Eugene never doubted that God spoke through His servant, Ellen White.

The visit of the ministers stretched into almost a week. Many victories were gained. After the adults had straightened out their lives, and by prayer and confession gained the victory over their sinful habits, God could use the Whites and Elder Andrews to help the young people. When an appeal was made for those who would follow Jesus all the way, seventeen children and youth arose and went forward.

"We want to be baptized and join the church," they said.

"Oh, but you can't be baptized now," they were told. "All the lakes and streams are frozen. Wait until spring."

Twelve of them were unwilling to wait.

"We'll cut a hole in the ice," they proposed. "No

one in Bible times had to wait six months to be baptized. Why should we?"

So the hole was cut, and one by one the twelve youth were lowered into the icy water and baptized.

When Elder and Mrs. White returned to Battle Creek after their two-month tour of the East, James White reported that they had traveled 3,200 miles by train and 600 miles by private conveyance. They had held 140 meetings, and Elder White had preached 60 times. John Andrews' program was also strenuous.

That spring the Whites moved onto a farm near Greenville, Michigan. Elder White needed to get away from the heavy burdens that pressed upon him in Battle Creek.

At the General Conference session held in 1867, Elder White turned over the presidency to Elder Andrews, who became the third president. Realizing his inexperience as an administrator, Elder Andrews leaned heavily on Elder and Mrs. White for counsel.

One day in 1868 Elder Andrews and J. O. Corliss, a younger minister, went to Greenville, where Elder White was slowly recovering his strength. They visited and prayed with the Whites.

"What can we do to draw our people closer together?" Elder Andrews asked. This had been a burden on his heart for some time.

"If we could have a camp meeting like those held back in the wonderful days of William Miller and his movement, it would have a unifying effect on our believers, I believe," said Elder White.

Elder Andrews was disturbed by the suggestion. He had heard of some Western camp meetings where there was shouting and sometimes wild disorder. A camp meeting dominated by that kind of spirit might damage the church in the eyes of other Christians, he pointed out.

Mrs. White assured him that the Lord would have His people draw together. A camp meeting could be a time of great blessing, she said.

Satisfied that this advice was good, Elder Andrews returned to Battle Creek, where he and his associates began planning for a camp meeting. They began searching for a suitable place, and found one in Wright's Grove in Ottawa County, Michigan. This was a maple, or sugar-bush, grove, as it was called in those days. Notices appeared in the *Review and Herald,* setting September 1-7 as the time for the meeting. The people were told what to bring in order to get the most out of the meetings.

"Most of all, bring a hungry heart," urged Elder Andrews. "Come up to this feast, brethren."

an EXPERIMENT

MANY PEOPLE came to the camp meeting, traveling by horse and buggy or ox team. Some came to the nearest town by train, and then walked the rest of the way. Tents were quickly erected.

These tents were brought by the various local churches, and all the members attending slept there. The roof and ends of each tent were made of cloth no thicker than present-day bed sheets, and a partition hung down the middle. The men of the church slept on one side, and the women on the other. Children slept wherever they could find a place.

Elder and Mrs. White arrived from their home in Greenville. With Elder Andrews, and the ordained ministers who were already on the grounds, Elder and Mrs. White met and prayed that God's richest blessings might be poured out upon the camp meeting.

The Whites walked around to inspect the grounds. There were two large tents, one of which contained straw for the mattresses and hay for the horses. The other tent was to be used in case of rain. Altogether, there were twenty-two church tents. Only one of these looked like the tents we have today. It was of canvas, and had been brought from New York State.

Many ministers were there and took part in the program, but the principal speakers were Elder and Mrs. White and Elder Andrews. Elder White spoke six times, Mrs. White five, and J. N. Andrews four times during the meetings.

The church members were delighted to meet old friends again, and even happier to greet some of the ministers whom they had known only through reading the *Review and Herald.* Some introduced themselves to Elders Bates, Cornell, Andrews, and others by saying, "Do you remember me? You baptized me at such and such a place so many years ago." Both ministers and converts were made happy by these reunions.

The meetings were held outdoors. Those attending sat on benches arranged under the trees. How they enjoyed the messages! They talked about them for months, especially one that Elder White began with the startling words: "It is court week in heaven, brethren. Have your cases ready!" This, of course, was a sermon on the judgment.

There were no electric lights in the camp. At various points stakes had been driven into the ground, and a box of dirt fastened on top of each of them. Torches consisting of pine knots were arranged in these boxes. When these knots were ignited they gave off quite a bit of light, and a fragrant odor.

Each night after the people had retired, a tall, brown-bearded man walked up and down the rows of tents. He stopped outside each tent and asked pleasantly, "Are you all comfortable for the night?"

If they said Yes, he went on to the next tent. If they needed water or matches or something else he could furnish, Elder Andrews supplied their needs. Thus the president of the General Conference took a fatherly interest in the campers at Wright's Grove.

On the third night there was a thunderstorm. Of course, the thin cloth tents didn't protect the campers from the rain, and there was no place to go to get dry. So everyone had to sleep as best he could. In the morning it was learned that the heavy canvas tent from New York hadn't leaked at all.

"We'll get canvas tents for the next camp meeting," the wet ones declared. Most of them did.

At the end of the week of meetings all attending were sorry to leave the sugar-bush grove where they had received so many blessings. Word spread rapidly of the success of that first camp meeting. Before the summer was over, meetings were also held in Clyde, Illinois, and Pilot Grove, Iowa.

God's servant, Mrs. White, had been right. The meetings had brought great blessings. Not only were the Adventists who attended blessed but also the hundreds of non-Adventists who had come in from the surrounding towns and farms were helped. After listening to the messages brought by the ministers, some of these visitors requested baptism.

The following year many camp meetings were held. Every conference held one, and the leaders had a hard time trying to staff them all. For many years the Michigan camp meeting was the largest and best attended. James and Ellen White, with Elder Andrews, attended these meetings. It took up their whole summer.

After describing the camp meeting at Wright's Grove, a writer concluded by remarking, "The preaching of Brother J. N. Andrews was with great power. He has accompanied Brother and Sister White much in their late tours among the churches, and has caught the same spirit."

James White was not happy with this statement. Three weeks later he wrote in the *Review:* "A recent writer, speaking of the Wright Camp meeting, . . . spoke of Brother Andrews as having labored with Brother and Sister White till he had caught the same spirit. Brother Andrews is a man of God. He is a close Bible student. He talks with God, and shares largely of the Holy Spirit direct from the throne. Brother and Sister White . . . often find relief in counselling with Brother Andrews, and listening to words of wisdom from his lips."

John Andrews' faith in Ellen White and her prophetic gift grew stronger all the time. During four months of travel with her husband and Elder Andrews Mrs. White wrote more than a thousand pages by hand. When she was writing she knew little of what was going on around her. This was strikingly illustrated at one camp meeting.

Elder Andrews was the speaker. Directly below the platform on which he stood, Ellen White sat at a table with her writing materials. All during the sermon she was writing. That noon, as they were eating lunch, one of the brethren asked Mrs. White what she thought of Elder Andrews as a preacher.

She replied that because it had been some time since she had heard him speak, it would not be exactly fair of her to pass judgment. She had not heard a word of his sermon, although it was spoken directly over her head.

Elder Andrews' family continued to live in Rochester at their home at 313 Main Street. At the time of the first camp meeting Charles was 10 years old. All signs of his old foot complaint had gone. Little Mary too lived to brighten the home. She was the pride and joy of John's heart. Other children were born to the Andrews family, but they died in infancy.

In 1869 James White and John Andrews changed places. Elder White again became the president of the

General Conference, a position he was to hold for two years. Elder Andrews became editor of the *Review and Herald.* Uriah Smith, another editor of the church paper, went out into the field for a time. This arrangement did not last long. Soon Elder Smith was back behind his desk in the *Review* building in Battle Creek. Elder Andrews was elected president of the New York Conference. Now he was most gratified because he could live in Rochester with his wife and children. One of the heaviest crosses Angeline had to carry was separation from her husband for long periods of time, but she carried it bravely.

Although he was a conference president, John Andrews was not tied to an office desk. Each summer he went out with a tent and held evangelistic meetings.

In 1872 a heavy sorrow came to John. His beloved wife, Angeline, died. She had been feeble for some time and on February 17 was stricken with paralysis. One arm became useless, and she could not speak. As a result of prayers offered in her behalf, the pain in her arm was greatly lessened.

One month later, on March 18, she was stricken again and died the following morning. She was 48 years old. Sorrowfully, John and the children followed the funeral procession to the Mount Hope Cemetery, where Angeline was laid to rest. The bereaved father was left to care for 14-year-old Charles and 10-year-old Mary.

For weeks Elder Andrews was prostrated with grief. His old friend John Loughborough wrote him a letter from California, seeking to comfort him. Elder White likewise sent his deepest sympathy. He recovered from the shock of Angeline's passing very slowly. To occupy his mind, he plunged into the great task of revising and enlarging his book *History of the Sabbath,* which had been published in 1861.

He decided to leave Rochester, which held so many memories of Angeline for him. He wanted to live near a good library where he could find the sources he needed for his book. So he and the children moved to South Lancaster, Massachusetts, where he rented a house near the academy. The children attended school, and John continued his research in nearby Boston.

At the request of Elder Andrews, Elder Uriah Smith, who had married Angeline's sister, Harriet, joined his brother-in-law in Massachusetts. Smith, also a scholar, worked with John Andrews on his *History of the Sabbath* project for more than a year. The resulting manuscript was so large that it was printed in three volumes. This work is still the most comprehensive treatment of the subject presently available.

Later, when Elder Andrews was called to Battle Creek to attend a meeting, the General Conference Committee asked him to study the question of Christian education and to bring some suggestions and recommendations that would help the church begin a truly Seventh-day Adventist college. This he did, and the statement he drew up proved of great value when Battle Creek College was founded.

But by now the Lord had another great and important task for His faithful servant.

a
CALL
from
EUROPE

DURING THE late 1850's and early 1860's, events were taking place in Europe that were to profoundly affect Elder Andrews as he accepted a new type of responsibility in a country beyond the sea. To understand the significance of these developments, we must transport ourselves to Poland and watch from an antichamber of a bishop's palace.

"Your excellency, Michael Czechowski is waiting to speak with you."

The bishop laid down his pen with an air of irritation. This was the third time the young Polish priest had asked for an interview.

"Very well. Show him in."

The secretary disappeared and soon returned, followed by a young man. Standing before the bishop, he bowed his head and flexed his knees. Then he waited for the bishop to speak.

"Very well, Czechowski, what is your problem?"

"Reverend Father, would you explain to me why we have images in our churches when they are forbidden by the Holy Scriptures?" Czechowski lifted his hand, and for the first time the bishop noticed the Bible he was holding.

"Where did you get that book?" he asked.

"A man was selling them in the market place, so I bought it."

"Don't you know that only the church has the power to say what the Bible means? If the church has uplifted these images there are good reasons, and you need not worry about what they are."

The bishop picked up his pen, intending to show that the interview was over. But the priest was not satisfied.

"Excuse me, sir, but I have another question. Why do so many of our priests get drunk when Saint Paul in his letter to Timothy says they should be sober?"

"I have no time to listen to your questions. I have important work to do. Take your endless questions to the pope!" With a wave of his hand the bishop dismissed the young priest.

"That's just what I'll do," said Czechowski to himself. A short time later he was actually on his way to Rome to see the pope.

Arriving at the city, he began asking various churchmen for permission to talk with the pope. Strangely enough, the pope actually agreed to see and listen to Czechowski. The priest poured out all of his perplexities. Patting the young man on the shoulder, the pope replied: "Don't let the fact that some priests lead bad lives cost you your faith in the church. Remember, one of the twelve disciples was very wicked."

Czechowski was not satisfied, and continued arguing with church officials in Rome. Finally, the chief secretary offered him an important position in Jerusalem, with an excellent salary. Realizing that they simply wanted to get rid of him, Czechowski declined the offer and sadly returned to his own country.

Completely disheartened, the priest decided to go
to Canada and start life anew there. In Montreal he attended various Protestant churches and, as a result,
was baptized. He married and reared a family. For a
while he preached to the French people in Montreal
and other cities. But the pay was very small. Anxious
to make a better home and living for his family, he
entered the United States and settled in Ohio.

In the town of Findlay he attended a series of
meetings held by Elder G. W. Holt and was baptized
into the Seventh-day Adventist Church. With Pastor
D. T. Bourdeau, a French Adventist minister, he
worked for six years among the French people in New
England and Quebec. But Czechowski could not forget the people of Europe who knew nothing of the
Adventist faith. He longed to help them.

As early as 1864 he asked the General Conference
to send him to Europe as a missionary for the church.
The brethren hesitated. Czechowski didn't seem to
know how to handle money. He was constantly in
debt. The General Conference itself was only one
year old, and there was little money in the treasury.
It hardly seemed possible that they could establish a
mission in Europe. Reluctantly, they turned down his
request.

Czechowski was not a man who became discouraged easily. He refused to accept the decision. He
was determined to go to Europe. Finally he went to
the headquarters of the First-day Adventists, where
he offered himself as their missionary to Europe.
They accepted him and purchased steamer tickets for
him to go to Europe. Arriving there, he began to
preach the doctrines of the Seventh-day Adventists
among the Waldenses in Northern Italy. Here
Katherine Ravel, his first convert, began to keep the
Sabbath.

He went on to Switzerland, where he raised up a church in Tramelan, baptizing his converts by night because of the bitter opposition of the local people. He stayed there for two years, spreading his faith in a paper he published, called the *Everlasting Gospel.*

Although he continued to preach the Bible Sabbath, for some reason he never told his converts that there was a church in America whose members observed the seventh-day Sabbath. Nor did he tell the First-day Adventists that he was actually teaching the people to observe Sabbath, rather than Sunday.

Leaving Tramelan, Czechowski traveled on into Eastern Europe, settling in Romania. Here he continued to preach.

One day, after Czechowski had left Switzerland, Albert Vuilleumier, one of the leaders of the Tramelan church, was looking over papers that the preacher had left behind. He came across a copy of the *Review and Herald.* Vuilleumier read this paper and was astonished to learn of the Seventh-day Adventist Church and its headquarters in Battle Creek. He immediately wrote to James White, who replied by inviting him to attend the coming General Conference session. Vuilleumier couldn't go himself, so he sent James Erzberger, a faithful German Sabbathkeeper.

Erzberger found his mission difficult. He arrived in New York with an English vocabulary consisting of little more than "J. N. Andrews, Battle Creek," printed on a card he carried. Somehow he bought a ticket and safely arrived at his destination. He was guided to the home of Elder Andrews. A short time later he became a member in the home of the James White family.

Three dedicated people began to teach Erzberger English, each teacher spending four hours a day with the eager pupil. So successful were their efforts that at the end of five weeks Erzberger was able to give a ten-minute talk in English.

Letters from the Adventists in Switzerland continued to arrive. During the fifteen months Erzberger spent in the United States the letters continued to plead for a missionary. J. N. Andrews was deeply moved by these continual appeals. As early as the 1870 General Conference session he was asking the question, "What can we do for Switzerland?"

Before he sailed back to Europe, Erzberger spent a number of weeks studying English at the home of Elder Andrews. The next European Adventist to visit in the United States was Ademar Vuilleumier, who stayed for four years.

From Vuilleumier, Elder Andrews learned of the difficulties the Swiss brethren were having in trying to find work that would permit them to keep the Sabbath. Some of the brethren were skilled watchmakers. A plan was therefore worked out whereby they would make watches and send them to J. N. Andrews, who would dispose of them retail in the United States. The church paper carried a notice of this project, and as a result, requests for watches came to Elder Andrews from many parts of the country. The Swiss Sabbathkeepers deeply appreciated the help Elder Andrews thus gave them.

The decision to send a missionary from America to Europe was not made hastily. Many meetings were held, and the problem was thoroughly discussed. In November, 1873, Elder George I. Butler, president of the General Conference, wrote in the *Review,* "There has been considerable said in the *Review* in regard to Bro. J. N. Andrews' going to Switzerland this season to look after the wants of the cause there." A few weeks later, James White wrote, "Elder Andrews is expected to go to Europe soon." That "soon" was to stretch out for another nine months.

Deeply interested as he was in the project, Andrews did not find it easy to respond to the call when it finally came. For two years he had enjoyed the peaceful seclusion of his home in South Lancaster. Charles and Mary were doing well in the academy. With free access to the libraries of Boston and of Harvard University, he had been able to do research there in revising his important book *History of the Sabbath.*

With his love of quiet study and writing, he hesitated to leave his pleasant home, prepare to master two or three new languages, cross the ocean, and plunge into the task of really launching the work in Europe. He was no organizer, and he shrank from the difficulties he saw would beset him.

It was not until the General Conference session held in Battle Creek in August, 1874, that the official call came for Elder Andrews to go to Europe as the first Seventh-day Adventist overseas missionary. Believing as he did in church organization, he accepted the decision of his brethren. While he sat in session with them as the official vote was taken, a strange transformation seemed to come over him.

"Elder Andrews, who had never before appeared so solemn, at once seemed altered in appearance. His face shone with such pronounced brightness that, as I saw him and heard his apparently inspired words of quiet contentment to be anywhere with the Lord, I thought of the story of Stephen and his wonderful experience before the Jewish Sanhedrin." Thus wrote Elder J. O. Corliss, who was present on that momentous day when the church first launched out into a worldwide missionary program.

With Charles, now 16, and Mary, 12, John Andrews went to Boston, where he was joined by Ademar Vuilleumier, who was returning to Switzerland to serve as translator for Elder Andrews until such time as he could master French. Ademar agreed to hold daily classes in French with the Andrews children while they crossed the ocean.

On Tuesday, September 15, the steamship *Atlas* sailed out of Boston harbor bound for Liverpool. James White reported this historic departure in the *Review and Herald:*

"Elder J. N. Andrews, who has nobly defended the truth from his very youth, leaves for Europe. . . . God bless him."

As John Andrews and his children stood on deck watching the shores of their beloved homeland disappear in the west, Charles asked, "When will we see our country again?"

"There is no way of knowing," replied his father. "It may be many years."

The voyage to England took twelve days. They reached Liverpool on a Saturday night. The ship was not unloaded on Sunday, so they had to remain on board until Monday. After clearing their baggage they bought train tickets for London, two hundred miles south of Liverpool. The train journey was most enjoyable. The visitors especially noticed the lovely green countryside, the neatly cultivated gardens, and the hedges that surrounded them.

In London, Elder Andrews and his group were met at the station by Elder W. M. Jones, a man who had accepted the Sabbath while visiting in the United States. Jones arranged for Elder Andrews to make a quick trip to Scotland to visit six isolated Sabbath-keepers there. Then it was back to London, down to Newhaven by train, and onto a boat that took them across the English Channel. On October 14 they traveled by train from Dieppe to Paris, where they took hotel rooms.

The last lap of the long journey was made the following day when they boarded the train for Neuchâtel, Switzerland. This town, which was near the French border, was to be their home for the next two years.

a NEW WAY of LIFE

IT WAS nearly noon when the train from Paris, carrying J. N. Andrews and his children, Charles and Mary, and Ademar Vuilleumier, pulled into the station at Neuchâtel. As they alighted they were happy to see the smiling faces of Ademar's two brothers, Albert and Luke, who extended a warm welcome to the American missionaries. The luggage was piled into a carriage, then the party was driven to the Vuilleumier home, where they found lunch ready for them.

Elder Andrews was surprised to see articles of food on the table that, as a faithful health reformer, he had long since discarded. But he made no comment at the time.

The next Sabbath Elder Andrews was asked to preach. He spoke on the rise of the Advent Movement, dwelling particularly on the work of Elder and Mrs. White and Joseph Bates. Since he spoke in English, Ademar Vuilleumier interpreted. The company was small, because most of the Swiss believers lived in other communities, particularly in the east. But those present showed great interest in the message.

The Vuilleumier house was large, and the Andrews family were given an apartment of their own. Charles never forgot the thrill he felt when he stood on the apartment balcony and looked out over the city. Not far away the waters of Lake Neuchâtel sparkled in the sunlight. On the opposite shore, apparently rising directly out of the lake, towered the mighty snow-capped Alps. Someday, Charles vowed, he would scale those mountains.

As the result of a family council, it was decided it would be most profitable for Elder Andrews to spend most of his time mastering the French language and teaching it to his children. Mary would be in charge of the kitchen. She would prepare the meals, while Charles would purchase the food supplies.

The morning came when the Andrews family set up housekeeping for themselves. Elder Andrews gave Charles a small sum of money and sent him to the market with the instruction that he was to buy the cheapest food available. The young man returned an hour later with some potatoes, one small cabbage, a bunch of turnips, and some apples and oranges.

"I could hardly understand a word the people said," he grumbled. "Brother Vuilleumier taught me some French on the boat, but these people talk so fast I couldn't catch on to what they were saying. I think I'll have to learn market-place French."

Mary looked over the supplies Charles had bought.

"How am I ever to prepare a dinner with food like this?" she asked, looking down into the market basket. "You didn't even bring any milk!"

"I asked Ademar about milk," Charles explained, "and he said the milkman will bring his cow and milk it right here at our front door."

Getting bread for the family proved a real problem. Hardly any of the people baked their own, because their stoves had no ovens. Bread was produced by the town bakers, who carried it around fresh every morning and sold it from door to door. Unfortunately, all they had to offer was white bread.

"Try to get some whole-wheat bread," Elder Andrews told Charles. "If there is none buy some graham flour, and we'll make brown porridge."

But Charles could find no whole-wheat bread or graham flour either. All during that winter, and for many years to follow, the diet of the missionaries was impoverished. They ate lots of white bread because it was the cheapest food available. During certain seasons it was almost impossible to find fruit and vegetables. Much of the ill health suffered by the family can be traced to poor dietary habits. They also found the climate extremely damp and cold. For weeks at a time there was no sunshine.

Shortly after arriving in Neuchâtel, Elder Andrews and his interpreter visited the Adventist companies throughout Switzerland. Most of these groups were small, made up of from eight to twelve persons. But they were very happy to meet the minister from the United States. They had almost no Adventist literature in the French language, and Elder Andrews longed to be able to give them truth-filled tracts and pamphlets.

James Erzberger, who had watched over the Adventist Church in Europe for four years, was particularly happy to have Elder Andrews in Switzerland. One day he brought exciting news.

"Do you know, Elder Andrews, that there is a company of Sabbathkeepers in Elberfeld, in Prussia?"

"No, I didn't know it. How did you hear about them?"

"A beggar came to my door asking for shelter for the night. I invited him in, and during the evening, as we visited, I tried to plant some seeds of truth in his mind. When I told him of the seventh-day Sabbath, he became excited. He told me that in Elberfeld, his home area, there is a group of German Christians who keep Saturday as their holy day."

"We must go and see them," said Elder Andrews. "Can you leave what you are doing? I'll put Albert Vuilleumier in charge here. You can translate for me into German."

After a two-day train trip, the men arrived at Elberfeld. They made a few inquiries and were directed to the home of the leader of the Sabbathkeeping group. Much to their joy, they learned that forty-six people were keeping the Sabbath. These good people had thought they were the only Sabbathkeeping Christians in all the world.

There was only one hall in the town. Elder Andrews hired it for a night and invited all the townspeople to attend. As he began to speak, he was surprised to see people sitting at tables scattered all over the hall, smoking and drinking beer. They continued to do this all through the service. Still, they were apparently much interested in what the speaker had to say.

In an account published in the *Review and Herald,* Andrews wrote, "If this wasn't a good place, it was at least a poor one, and that was better than none at all."

At a smaller meeting with the believers, Andrews talked about systematic benevolence, and they gladly agreed to support the work of the church in this way. They took up a collection large enough to repay the visitors for what they had spent on their trip to Elberfeld. Elder Andrews spent five weeks with this company, then returned to Neuchâtel, leaving Erzberger to teach them more fully.

In general the work went very slowly. Members entered the church by two's and three's. In early August, 1875, less than a year after arriving in Switzerland, Elder Andrews baptized eight persons in the waters of Lake Neuchâtel. But how he longed for more workers. He wrote to the *Review and Herald,* "I beg then for strong young men in the cause of Christ. I beg with tears for men, true-hearted men of God, to enter this great harvest field."

Toward the end of the year good news came. A French minister, Elder D. T. Bourdeau, with his wife, was coming to Europe to assist Elder Andrews. This was the man who had worked with Czechowski many years before.

It was the hope of the General Conference that Bourdeau would relieve Elder Andrews of some of his burdens. When Bourdeau arrived in Neuchâtel, John took him around and introduced him to every Sabbathkeeping group in Switzerland.

John Andrews' heart was thrilled by the prospect of raising up companies of believers in the many countries of Europe. With increased diligence he applied himself to learning both French and German.

"My first important work here is to become master of the French language so as to speak it correctly," he wrote to Elder White. "It is not a light task to accomplish this. I have toiled early and late, and have made some progress. . . . It is now the great desire of my heart to preach Christ in the French language with freedom and see sinners converted."

Charles and Mary likewise realized their need of knowing French. It was a strange experience for them to walk down the streets of the town and hear people speaking, yet not be able to understand what they were saying. Charles talked to his father about this.

"You and Mary must learn French just as soon as possible," said Elder Andrews.

"Do you mean we must attend a French school?"

"No, I'll do what I can to teach you French, and

Elder Vuilleumier will help also. But if we are really
going to learn the language, there's only one way to
do it, and that is to exclude the use of English in our
home."

"How can we do that?" asked Mary. "That's the
only language I can speak well."

"From now on," explained her father, "English
will be permitted for just one hour each day, and that
is from five to six in the evening."

"That will make a game out of it," laughed
Charles.

But it wasn't easy. Sometimes the children would
tingle with excitement as they tried to describe something interesting and found their knowledge of
French insufficient. They were soon carrying their
English-French dictionary wherever they went. Sometimes they just waited for their English hour in the
evening, then talked as fast as they could.

It was a difficult program, but the three of them
did indeed learn French. Two years after arriving in
Neuchâtel, Mary was speaking the language like any
French girl, according to one of the French workers
in the office. By 1876 they were ready to tackle German. English was then completely banished from the
home, and the family spoke only French and German, even among themselves.

By then Elder Andrews felt ready to begin preaching and writing in French. His main interest was in
discovering the best way to carry the message to every town and village in Switzerland, and, ultimately,
to all Europe. In order to explore the possibilities,
he called the leaders of the companies together. He
wished to know whether methods used in the United
States would prove equally successful in Europe.

"Could we hold tent meetings in different places?"
he asked. "Would the people come?"

The brethren shook their heads.

"*It would never work!* You have no idea how strong the state church is here. One word to the townspeople from their pastors and they would become uncontrollable. In no time they would come and tear your tent to pieces."

"Could we hire a hall in each town and hold services there?" was his next question.

Again they shook their heads.

"In most towns the city hall is the only large gathering place besides the church. The authorities would never permit you to use it. Even in the large cities where there are private halls you would find trouble. Should a man rent you such a hall the priest would warn the people against him, and no one would do business with him. He'd soon be in real trouble."

"Then what shall we do? What can we do?" asked Elder Andrews. He was beginning to wonder whether there was *any* way to break down the barriers.

"There is one sure way to reach the people. If you will print a small paper, we can send it through the mails. Then the priests won't be able to keep the people from learning the truth."

"Printing a paper would be very expensive," remarked Elder Andrews. "Could we take subscriptions before printing so we would know how many would pay for such a paper?"

"No. That may be possible in your country, but not here. Swiss law says that you may send a paper or magazine to anyone. If he returns the paper it means he doesn't want it. If he accepts the paper for four or five times, that means he wants it. Then you hand the name and address to the government. They collect the subscription from the man and send it to you. You can get names and addresses from the town register."

"Suppose we find the subscriptions aren't coming

in fast enough to support the paper. Could we suspend it for a couple of months then print again?"

There was a chorus of protest. It seemed as though everyone was trying to speak at once. One of the leaders explained why this wouldn't work.

"If we print three or four issues, then stop the paper for a few weeks, our enemies will laugh and say to the people, 'See, it is not permanent. Just let them alone, and soon it will die of itself!' No. Once we have started the paper, we must print it regularly."

Having listened to all the advice, Elder Andrews decided to begin printing a little paper in French. So shortly after this meeting he carried the first manuscript for a small pamphlet to the printers. When he returned to collect the copies he was dismayed. In some places they had used too much ink and the papers were badly smudged. On other copies the print was so pale the pages were almost impossible to read. His associates agreed with him that the printing plant in Neuchâtel couldn't do the quality of work they required.

"Then where shall we go?" asked Elder Andrews. One of the brethren had the answer.

"I understand that the best printing in the country is done in the city of Basel," he remarked. Elder Bourdeau said this was true. So he and Elder Andrews decided they must move to Basel and have the printing done there.

Shortly after arriving in Neuchâtel, Elder Bourdeau had written to the *Review and Herald* expressing the hope that a French paper might be started soon.

"I expect to take charge of the paper and thus leave Elder Andrews free to preach and travel."

Unfortunately, this plan didn't work. Elder Bourdeau's real talent was more for evangelistic than editorial work. His knowledge of French grammar was not so detailed or extensive as that of Elder Andrews. Although French was his native language, Bourdeau was not as fluent a writer as his companion, who had dug it all out of books.

When Andrews saw that Bourdeau's heart was not in office work he gave him his blessing and sent him out to preach.

But when would Elder Andrews be able to preach among the French people, winning souls for the kingdom? He felt tied to his desk.

Soon encouraging word came from Battle Creek. James White was thrilled by the reports from Europe.

"Come, brethren," Elder White wrote in his characteristic way, "the cause of God in Europe needs help. Let's raise ten thousand dollars for this project. I will give five hundred." His wife gave a similar amount.

Money rolled in, and by early 1877, $8,000 had already been raised and sent to Elder Andrews. Perhaps even more important than the money received was the knowledge that the church at home was praying for him.

Like Paul of old, John Andrews "thanked God and took courage."

LAUNCHING the PAPER

ELDER ANDREWS decided to call his paper *Les Signes des Temps*, which would be "The Signs of the Times" in English. Already he had published a number of tracts in French, German, and Italian, but now the French-speaking people would have a regular paper of their own.

It was a thrilling moment for this great scholar when he picked up the pen to write his first article for the *Signes*. When he had finished he read it aloud to make sure it was clear and understandable. He invited Elder Bourdeau to write and also Louis Aufranc, a recent convert and an enthusiastic worker. When the material for the paper was all assembled John handed it to his 14-year-old daughter, Mary.

"Look these over," he told her, "and make any corrections you think necessary to make it read perfect French." He had great confidence in his daughter.

Mary spent several hours working on the articles. There were very few changes needed in her father's articles. But although the other two spoke French as their mother tongue, they hadn't mastered the French grammar as Elder Andrews and Mary had. Their articles needed considerable revision.

The material was next taken to one of the best publishers in Basel. That first edition numbered 2,000 copies. Many prayers were offered before the papers were mailed out. When letters began to arrive from people interested in the *Signes* and its message, the hearts of Elder Andrews and his fellow workers sang for joy!

John Andrews soon learned that unless he personally supervised the printing, serious mistakes would creep in. He didn't want people to laugh at the *Signes,* so when the paper went to press he was there. One day some small dots appeared along the side of the paper. Andrews stopped the press no less than fifty times as he sought to get rid of those dots.

Another time, as Elder Andrews was reading proof sheets he discovered that an accent mark was missing from a word on the front page. With his pen he indicated the error and sent the proofs back to the printer. For some reason the man failed to see the correction, and the entire edition carried the mistake. When this was called to the attention of the printer he suggested throwing the defective copies away. Realizing that to do so would cost an extra forty dollars, which would prove a heavy blow to the struggling workers, Elder Andrews personally wrote in the accent mark on each of the three thousand copies. It took him all of one day and far into the night.

Sometimes Elder Andrews had problems with his writers. One morning he was looking over an article prepared by Louis, later Dr. Aufranc, dealing with the change of the Sabbath. He had written that the early Christians had put Saturday in the place of Sunday.

Not wishing to correct this without the author's consent, Elder Andrews asked Brother Aufranc to drop by his office. Brother Bourdeau came with him, and they talked about the paper. Then Andrews picked up the article and asked whether Dr. Aufranc hadn't written just the opposite of what he really wanted to say.

"No," said Elder Bourdeau, "that is how it should be written in French." Elder Andrews threw up his hands.

"Then I despair of ever learning French," he exclaimed.

Brother Aufranc thought for a couple of minutes. Then he said, "I have committed an error."

Elder Bourdeau finally also agreed that Andrews was right. The article was corrected and sent to the printers. Had the article appeared as Brother Aufranc had written it, the statement would have been most confusing.

Every morning Charles placed a pile of letters on his father's desk. They came from all parts of Europe, as well as from the United States. As the paper went out to an ever-increasing number of subscribers this mail became steadily heavier. The missionary was particularly pleased to know that his tracts and the paper were being given to French people in Canada and the United States, and a number were beginning to keep the Sabbath.

All day long, from dawn until far into the night, Elder Andrews labored to care for this growing correspondence. He wrote many articles for *Les Signes*, as well as supervising its printing and distribution. He also continued writing for the *Review and Herald.*

During a period of seven years he wrote more than 480 articles, an average of five or six each month. He was also studying, and his brilliant mind continued to explore the wonders of God's Word.

Rumors circulated that Elder Andrews had memorized the whole Bible. A friend asked him about it one day.

"John, I hear you can repeat the whole Bible from memory, is that so?"

Elder Andrews smiled.

"So far as the New Testament is concerned, if it was obliterated, I could reproduce it word for word; but I would not say as much for the Old Testament."

Not satisfied with reading the Bible in English only, he read it with clear understanding in French, German, Italian, Greek, Latin, and Hebrew.

One day, after *Les Signes* had been going out for three or four months, Elder Andrews received a letter postmarked Naples, Italy. Who can this be? asked Elder Andrews. So far as he knew, there wasn't a Sabbathkeeper in southern Italy. With great interest he read the letter. It was from a man named Ribton. This man, who was a medical doctor, had received a copy of *Les Signes* from Elder Jones, the Adventist minister who had met Andrews in London. He read it carefully and came to the conclusion that the seventh day of the week is the true Bible Sabbath.

"I am convinced that you are right," he wrote, "and I have begun to keep the Sabbath. My wife and daughter are doing the same, and we have another lady here who is following our example. Please come and baptize us."

"Praise the Lord!" exclaimed Elder Andrews. "Here is a witness for God right in the land of papal darkness."

He wrote Dr. Ribton that his many duties made it impossible for him to go to Naples immediately, but he promised that he would visit them just as soon as possible.

Meanwhile, the paper was costing more than Andrews had expected. If there was one thing he hated more than another, it was to have to ask for money. He would rather go without necessary food and clothing than to write to the General Conference asking for funds. When he went to Europe the brethren didn't set any specific salary for him. They wanted to find out how living costs there would compare with those in the United States.

So, instead of setting a salary, they agreed to send him money from time to time. Unfortunately, during the first two or three years those times were few and far between. To publish tracts and pamphlets, and later on *Les Signes,* Andrews had to go into debt for three or four months at a time. Little by little he withdrew his own money from the bank and used it to meet living expenses. Sometimes he was several months behind with his rent.

Faced with the expenses of a trip to Italy to see Dr. Ribton, Andrews wrote a letter to Elder James White, "If you think proper to do so—send me $500 or $1,000." Ellen White read this letter, and beneath the signature she wrote and underlined, "Please send immediately."

James White knew that Elder Andrews would need more and more money, so he made another appeal in the *Review* for the expanding work in Europe. This brought in $2,000. And the General Conference committee voted to raise $10,000, but it was many months before this money arrived in Europe.

On January 13, 1877, John Andrews was struck down with pneumonia. He would shake with cold chills, then he would perspire with burning fever. After this had continued for a week, a doctor was called. He gave the minister a thorough examination.

After he had finished, the physician pointed to the minister's gaunt face and exclaimed, "This man is almost starved to death!" It was all too true. In order to

have money to use for the work, Andrews had often
gone without necessary food. His temperature continued to rise, and he lost consciousness. For many days
he was very sick. Then gradually he began to recover.

Dr. Ribton wrote encouraging letters. He was prac-
ticing medicine just enough to support his family.
His burning desire was to spread the truth he had
come to love. He sometimes made as many as fifteen
or twenty missionary calls in a single week. Wherever
he found people who could read French he sent them
copies of *Les Signes.*

"We must have a paper in Italian," he wrote to
Elder Andrews. Poor John! He didn't know how to
answer. Elder Erzberger had never stopped begging
for a paper in German. How could he publish journals
in three languages every month?

Elder Andrews' serious illness had made it necessary for him to postpone his trip to Italy. But with the
coming of summer he decided to make the journey.
He bought a third-class ticket and boarded the train.
It was difficult to sleep on the unpadded board bench,
but he rejoiced that by doing so he might save a few
dollars for the cause of God. Dr. Ribton met him in
Naples and took him to his home. The minister was
perfectly satisfied with Dr. Ribton's understanding of
the Bible. It was also evident that the wife, daughter,
and one other woman were also ready for baptism.

There was no church in the city that they could
use for this service, so Andrews and his four candi-
dates went to a beach near the small town of Puteoli.
There, in the sparkling waters of the Mediterranean,
he baptized the new believers. That afternoon the five
partook of the Lord's Supper together.

Dr. Ribton was extremely eager for Elder Andrews
to hold meetings in Naples. But first they had to find
a place. They tried to rent one of the churches in the

city. There were several Protestant churches in Naples, but not one would open its doors to the visitor from Switzerland. Finally, the owner of an apartment house said they might hold a quiet meeting in the large parlor.

The doctor visited a number of his friends, neighbors, and former patients, telling them about the meeting and inviting them to attend. At the appointed hour a few interested persons strolled into the building, brought more by curiosity than by a desire to study a new religion.

Unfortunately, some enemies had been watching Dr. Ribton and were determined to break up his meeting. First they stationed four young men on the sidewalk outside the apartment house. These pretended to be assisting the Adventist minister by calling out to the passers-by, "Come inside. There is a Protestant meeting going on here, and the clergyman is going to expose the evil deeds of the pope."

Naturally, members of the state church were irritated. They tramped into the parlor, talked loudly, and interrupted the speaker. At the same time others slipped into the building and went up and down the halls, pushing Protestant tracts under the apartment doors. The residents understandably became very angry. They rushed down into the parlor and helped to break up the meeting.

The apartment-house owner then said he could no longer let them use his building. So Elder Andrews and Dr. Ribton had to go from house to house, looking for those who would listen to them as they read and explained the Word of God.

Elder Andrews spent five weeks with the Ribton family in Naples. On August 6 he bade them farewell and proceeded to Torre Pellice, the principal Waldensian town, in northern Italy. Here he visited

with Mrs. Catherine Revel, the woman who had kept
the Sabbath all alone ever since hearing Czechowski
preach nearly fifteen years before.

Then he took a train that went through the famous
eight-mile-long Mount Cenis Tunnel under the Alps,
then across Switzerland, and home to Basel.

Back in Battle Creek, James White was thinking
that if Elder Andrews was going to print papers in
French, German, and Italian he would need more
help. He pointed this out to the General Conference
committee, and they voted to send Mr. and Mrs.
William Ings and Sister Maud Sisley to Basel to join
Elder Andrews and his family. Since Brother Ings
was a printer, his help would be particularly valuable.

At first Elder Andrews saw problems connected
with the arrival of these new workers. Would the new-
comers expect to live in the house occupied by the
Andrews family? If not, there would be more furni-
ture to buy. Would they be willing to sacrifice and
get along with the barest necessities in order to save
money for the work? But his real concern was that
the atmosphere of the establishment would be maintained.

"I fear we shall be overwhelmed with English,"
he wrote. "We are trying to shut it out of the house
and speak only French and German."

But these new workers were devoted and proved
to be a great blessing to John Andrews and his children.

After their arrival it was decided to establish a
Seventh-day Adventist publishing house. No longer
would they have to depend on local presses. Brother
Ings took charge of the printing. He found a valuable
assistant in Charles Andrews. Mary continued to assist
her father with his editorial work, while Mrs. Ings
took over the cooking and housework.

At the beginning of 1878 it seemed that brighter days were ahead for the Adventist Church in Europe. The prospect brought joy to the heart of Elder Andrews. He did not dream of the heartache the new year would bring.

GATHERING CLOUDS

AT THE beginning of 1878 Elder Andrews hopefully looked into the future. He thanked God for the progress of the work and hoped for even better days ahead. There were now Sabbathkeepers in England, Scotland, Ireland, Egypt, Norway, Sweden, Denmark, Holland, Germany, Russia, France, and Italy.

Elder James White, president of the General Conference, was greatly encouraged by reports of the work in Europe, and he wrote to the brethren there: "We say to Elders Andrews, Bourdeau, Erzberger, Dr. Ribton, and others, Be of good cheer! . . . You have our prayers."

Then, addressing the believers in North America, Elder White went on to say, "While we pray let us act the part that God would have us act in the answer of our own prayers. . . . We have made an appeal for ten thousand dollars to support our missions in Europe besides the ten thousand already raised to establish the press in Switzerland." He and his wife promised to give a thousand dollars into this fund.

No wonder Elder Andrews could write from his office in Basel, "The course of truth is onward. Our Lord is coming. Our days of mourning will before long be ended. So we will labor and travail in hope of the life that shall never end."

Good reports continued to arrive from all parts of the European field. Dr. Ribton reported twenty-two Sabbathkeepers in Naples. He offered to spend his entire time preaching if he might receive a small salary, just sufficient to support his family. He was meeting fierce opposition, and there were threats that he would be killed if he continued to preach. Policemen had to be posted at the doors of the place where he was holding his meetings. One of the services was broken up when boys, paid by the local priest, tossed firecrackers in through open windows on a hot summer night.

Some time later Dr. Ribton wrote to Elder Andrews asking permission to go to Alexandria, Egypt. In this city, eighty thousand Italians made their homes, and Dr. Ribton proposed carrying the Sabbath truth to them. Andrews agreed and sent money for transporting the doctor and his family to that large Egyptian city.

One day there came to Elder Andrews' attention an especially needy missionary project, but he had absolutely no funds. He began to pray that in some way the Lord would provide the money.

Across the Atlantic, in Battle Creek, Ellen White had just been given a beautiful new silk dress. It had cost $45 and was a gift from a dear friend. Mrs. White greatly admired the dress, but had an impression that Elder Andrews was in need of money. So she took the dress to a Sabbathkeeping merchant and asked him to sell it for her. He turned over the money received, which amounted to $50, to Mrs. White. She promptly sent it to Elder Andrews, who wrote back that this was the very sum he had prayed for.

As the spring of 1878 moved into summer, a new,

perplexing problem began to trouble John Andrews.
His daughter, Mary, was not well. Little by little she
was losing strength. No longer could she work for
long hours in the publishing house. She developed a
persistent cough and found breathing difficult. Elder
Andrews took her to a local doctor. He pronounced
the dread word, consumption, or tuberculosis as it is
generally called today. John asked whether there was
hope for her recovery. The doctor shook his head;
there was no sure cure.

In September, Andrews received an invitation to
attend the coming General Conference session to be
held in Battle Creek. He decided to go and take Mary
to the Battle Creek Sanitarium. Surely his good friend
Dr. Kellogg would find some way to save a life so valuable to the work of God. Charles would remain with
Elder Ings and keep the presses rolling.

He wrote to the General Conference of his plans,
carefully pointing out that he would be responsible
for the entire cost of getting Mary to Battle Creek.

Elder Bourdeau had decided to return to America,
and would travel with him by the least expensive pas-
sage. There was so much work to be done before Andrews could leave Basel that he feared he might be
late for the conference.

By working night and day he managed to leave
enough prepared material for two complete issues of
Les Signes. Then he and Mary said good-by to
Charles and boarded the ship for America.

The General Conference session opened on October 4. Elder Andrews arrived in Battle Creek the
same day. In the afternoon he spoke to the assembled
delegates and the Battle Creek church members. As
he pointed out various countries in Europe that now
had Sabbathkeepers, the people were thrilled. They
marveled that he and his fellow workers had accom-

plished so much in just four years.

Elder Andrews lost no time in taking Mary to the Sanitarium, where Dr. Kellogg gave her a careful examination. The doctor was shocked to see how far the disease had progressed. Kindly and sadly he told John that, from a human standpoint, there was no hope for her recovery. She could not live for more than a month or two.

From that day on, the devoted father scarcely left Mary's bedside. Day and night he watched over her, doing for her everything that could make her comfortable. Dr. Kellogg warned Elder Andrews of the danger he was running that he might contract the disease himself. Nothing could persuade the father to leave the bedside of his loving, gifted daughter.

On the night of November 27, Mary Andrews died at the age of 17. She was buried in the Oak Hill Cemetery in Battle Creek. A few days after the funeral Elder Andrews received a comforting message from Ellen G. White:

"In my last vision, I saw you. Your head was inclined toward the earth, and you were following in tears your beloved Mary to her last dwelling place in this world. Then I saw the Lord looking upon you full of love and compassion. I saw the coming of Him who is to give life to our mortal bodies, and your wife and children came forth out of their graves clad in immortal splendor."

Elder Andrews found the loss simply overwhelming. For weeks he was prostrated with grief. So many of his plans for the work in Europe had centered in Mary. She had done the editorial work in the office, leaving him free to visit Sabbathkeepers in various parts of Europe.

Somehow he couldn't understand why he had been called to make such a sacrifice. To a long-time friend he wrote in his grief, "I seem to be having hold upon God with a numb hand." A year later he wrote in the *Review and Herald,* "Today is the anniversary of my daughter's death. I cannot tell why one who promised to be so useful should be taken away. God's judgments are a great deep."

He spent much of that winter in Battle Creek and was often invited to visit various churches to tell of his experiences in Europe. When he was able he always enjoyed doing this. Mrs. White urged him to remain in the United States until he rebuilt his own health. And when he returned, she said, he should take a good wife so that he and Charles would have a home again.

Poor Elder Andrews! Although Angeline had been dead for six years, he could not forget her long enough even to consider marrying again. He wrote to Mrs. White, thanking her for her interest in him and his happiness, but saying he could not follow her advice. No one knows what might have been the result if he could have brought himself to remarry. Perhaps he might have lived much longer and his usefulness to the cause of God might have been greatly increased.

In April, 1879, the new Battle Creek church was completed. It was called the Dime Tabernacle because people had been urged to donate a dime a week to pay for the building. It was the largest church in the city and could seat more than 3,000 persons.

On April 17 Elder Andrews preached the dedicatory sermon. Every seat was taken, and hundreds of people were turned away. Those who listened to him declared that he preached one of the greatest sermons they had ever heard.

In the spring Elder Andrews traveled more and more widely, visiting churches in Pennsylvania, New York, and other States. He went to Rochester, where

he and Angeline had spent eight happy years together.
All this time he was rejoicing in the reports that
reached him from William Ings in Basel. Although
the printer wrote encouragingly of the work, Elder
Andrews knew very well that he was greatly needed.

Traveling westward, he visited his aged mother,
still living in Waukon, and bade her farewell for what
he thought would be the last time. Then he went to
New York and in late May sailed for Europe on the
S.S. *Virginia.* He secured a first-class cabin for only
$55, a cheap fare even for those days.

The *Virginia* was to make only one more voyage.
On the very next trip, approaching the coast of Europe
in a dense fog, she ran aground and was lost. Nine of
the passengers were drowned.

Following a quiet crossing Andrews arrived in
Glasgow and, after a visit with friends, boarded the
train for London. Suddenly he was struck down by
his old enemy, chill fever. Although it was spring-
time and the weather was warm, he shook with chills
from head to foot.

Realizing that he might be in for a long siege of
sickness, he managed to board a train for Southampton, where his old friend and comrade, J. N. Loughborough, was working. The Loughborough home was
opened wide for the stricken leader. The chills gave
way to burning fever. Elder Loughborough and his
wife took tender care of the sick man, but it was three
months before he was well enough to continue his
journey to Basel. While staying with the Lough-
boroughs, Andrews was encouraged to learn that a
Turkish merchant had read a copy of *Les Signes* and
had begun to keep the Sabbath.

Elder Andrews never fully recovered his health
after that terrible siege in England. He managed to get
back to Basel, where he again took to his bed. From

his sickbed he dictated letters and articles for the paper, and in that room he transacted the business of the church.

Toward the end of 1879 the General Conference Committee decided to hold a general meeting in Basel for all the workers in Europe. To this conference they proposed to send Elders Haskell and W. C. White. In the end, only Elder Haskell was present. From the European field, Elders Matteson, Andrews, Loughborough, Erzberger, and others attended. At this gathering, held in 1880, Elder Andrews was placed in charge of the entire European field.

The Lord looked down in pity upon His afflicted servant and sent him encouragement in the form of a dream. This dream he described to Ellen White in a letter dated May 23, 1880:

"I dreamed of meeting you and the first question (I asked was), 'Have you seen anything about Switzerland?' You said, 'Yes. Only a few days ago I was shown that the angel Gabriel was sent to Basel to make inspection of things there.' I asked, 'What report did he give concerning me?'

"You answered, 'He said that you had been trying hard to do the work of the Lord.' "

Surely the Lord might well say concerning Elder Andrews, "He has done what he could."

BRIGHT SUNSET

THE HARDSHIPS suffered by Elder Andrews in his early years of work at Neuchâtel and Basel weakened his physical constitution. The powers of his mind, however, remained as strong as ever. He continued writing articles in English, French, German, and Italian, but tried to be more temperate in his work. Whenever possible he took long walks in the open country.

His interest in the European Adventist publications never waned; they continued to receive his first attention. It was in this that he missed the help of his daughter, Mary. There was no one to proofread the papers as she had done, so he took over the task himself. Even when he was feeling ill the proof sheets would be placed on his bed. Propped up on pillows, he would laboriously correct them.

It seemed that a miracle happened each month. As deadlines rolled around, Elder Andrews would have just enough strength to care for that particular issue of the paper. Then he would have to rest until time for the next issue, when he would again rally for the task.

Each morning someone would lay a writing board across his lap, and he would write as much as he could. There were days when he could write only one page, on other days only a few words. Once he spent ten days preparing one article for the *Review and Herald.* His physical condition continued to worsen.

Hoping that medical science might have discovered some remedy that would help him, Elder Andrews called in a local doctor. The man examined Andrews carefully and advised him to go to England for a time. A change in climate, said the doctor, might help him. So he went to Southampton, where John Loughborough was still working. Andrews found strength to help Loughborough pitch a tent and begin a series of evangelistic meetings. He enjoyed being with his fellow soldier and lifetime friend. But it turned out that Elder Loughborough had to do most of the speaking.

The change of climate was no help to Elder Andrews. An English doctor urged him to leave England and go to a dry climate. Feeling that his post of duty was in Switzerland, he sent for Charles, who came and escorted his father home.

John wondered whether he would ever be strong again. He sent for the same doctor who had examined him before. When the doctor came, the sick man reached out his hand and took that of the physician.

"Doctor," he said, "I want you to examine me again. Tell me what is really wrong with me. What can I do to regain my strength?" John was thinking of the warnings Dr. Kellogg had given him in Battle Creek when he was nursing Mary.

The doctor examined Andrews. His face was sober as he asked a question.

"You want the truth, I presume, Mr. Andrews."

"Yes, doctor."

"Then I must tell you that you are suffering from consumption. One lung is nearly gone, and the other

is infected too. I can hold out no hope for your recovery."

When the General Conference Committee learned
the condition of the stricken missionary they appointed a day of fasting and prayer on his behalf.
Elder Loughborough hurried to Switzerland. Ministers from the Swiss field also gathered around his
bedside, prayed, and anointed him.

The next step taken by the leaders of the church
was to send Elder S. N. Haskell to Switzerland. Elder
Haskell was a man of faith. It was felt that he might
be able to lift the spirits of the stricken missionary.
Elder Haskell came in the latter part of 1882. He was
instructed to take any steps he thought useful in
helping to preserve such a valuable life. After spending several weeks in Switzerland, Elder Haskell reported through the columns of the *Review:* "The re-
sults already accomplished through the efforts of
Elder Andrews are in some respects truly marvelous."

Elder Haskell was distressed when he found Elder
Andrews living in a house filled with books and
printing supplies. He discussed the situation with the
French brethren, and they agreed with him. In a
short time they found a more agreeable house. While
Elder Haskell took John on a pleasant one-day excur-
sion, the move was swiftly made. Elder Andrews returned to find to his astonishment that his living
quarters had been changed.

As time passed, Andrews came to feel more and
more that his very life was bound up with the prosperity of the work in Europe. He wrote to the *Review
and Herald,* "The burden upon my heart is so heavy
with regard to the advancement of the work in Europe that the turn things will take, whether for prosperity or adversity, will, I believe, decide whether I
shall live or die."

One day Elder Andrews received a parcel from an Adventist sister in California. It contained some foods hard to find in Europe. There were nuts and raisins, and packages of dried fruit—apricots, peaches, pears, and prunes. Other packages followed. He was deeply touched by the thoughtfulness of believers on the other side of the world whom he had never seen.

In the spring of 1883 Dr. Kellogg traveled from Battle Creek to Vienna, Austria, to attend some important medical lectures. On his way back to the United States he went to Basel to visit with Elder Andrews, whom he had known since boyhood. He found him in bed, and gave him a brief examination, which only confirmed the diagnosis made by the Swiss doctor.

Andrews explained to Kellogg his reasons for wanting so much to live longer. There were so many tasks still waiting. Prospects for the advance of the message all over Europe were growing brighter all the time. Then, pointing to a wooden chest in the corner of his room, he said, "Open that chest, doctor, and see what I have there."

Dr. Kellogg opened the chest. It contained scores of unfinished articles, pamphlets, and tracts.

"No one knows how to complete these except myself," he said. "If I die they will perish with me."

Dr. Kellogg did all he could for the sick man, then hastened back to the United States. There he appealed to the General Conference Committee to do everything in their power to help prolong the life of this man of God.

Andrews did not surrender to his weakness without a struggle. As late as May, 1883, he would dress and go downstairs to breakfast, his German Bible under his arm. Sinking into a chair, he would help himself to some food, then sit and stare at it.

"If I could only eat," he said to his companions

one morning, "I think I could write. But it won't go down."

Then he would lean his arms on the table while tears trickled down his thin cheeks and fell onto the table.

On July 22 he wrote in his diary, "Today I enter my fifty-fifth year. My life seems wholly filled with faults. I pray that I may be thoroughly cleansed in the blood of Christ."

Realizing that the time would soon come when Elder Andrews could no longer direct the work in Europe, the General Conference appointed Elder B. L. Whitney to go to Basel and prepare to take over. Someone suggested that John's aged mother, Sarah Andrews, go with Elder Whitney to be with her son. Before deciding, George I. Butler, president of the General Conference, wrote to Elder Andrews and asked his permission. At first John said he didn't wish his mother to come.

"I would rather not have her see me in my present feeble condition," he wrote. "It would only bring sorrow to her heart. If I must die, let it be alone."

Elder Butler wrote and explained to Elder Andrews that his mother would like nothing more than to be able to minister to her son. When Ellen White was asked about the move, she wrote to Elder Butler, "Sister Andrews should be with her son." Reluctantly John gave his consent.

When Elder Whitney sailed for Europe, Mother Andrews, Mrs. Martha Andrews, the widow of John's brother, William, and Martha's daughter, Sarah, were with him.

The arrival of this group in Basel in July did indeed bring comfort to the invalid. Elder Whitney immediately took charge of the publishing work, for Elder Andrews could no longer do so.

All during that summer Elder Andrews was troubled in mind. Why, he wondered, did God let him suffer so much? Why was he not healed and allowed to go on with the work he longed to do? The future seemed dark.

But with the coming of autumn a change came over him. He cast all his burdens on the Lord. Elder Vuilleumier, who kept a diary during those sad days, wrote on September 7: "He is calm and quiet. He feels the burden no more. Today . . . he touchingly said, 'I have reached a point which I compare with a vessel nearing port. It is no longer in midocean, open to the fury of the storms. The cliffs of the shore keep off the winds, the sea has become quiet, the waves vanish, the calm appears.' "

Thus he continued until October 21, when he expressed the hope that this might be his last day. At noon a little broth was brought to him, but he was unable to eat. He called for paper and pen, saying he had one last bit of writing to do. Wondering what it might be, the workers brought him the supplies requested. Then, with a trembling hand, he wrote a paragraph stating that he was donating his last $500 to the European Mission. Having accomplished this, he sank back exhausted onto the pillows.

In late afternoon, as they had done so many times, the workers gathered at the bedside of Elder Andrews to pray for their leader. Sarah Andrews sat by his head, gently fanning his face. They knelt and prayed. As they rose from their knees, the golden rays of the setting sun filled the room with glory. It was very quiet.

Albert Vuilleumier looked at Elder Andrews' face and exclaimed, "Why, he's dead!"

And so it was. He had fallen asleep so peacefully that no one knew when the moment of death had

come. The news was flashed by cable to the General
Conference. Later Elder Whitney was to write: "We
have sustained an irreparable loss."

In accordance with his written desire, no eulogy
appeared in the *Review and Herald* that announced
his death. But to the thousands who had been brought
into the church through the pen and voice of John
Nevins Andrews, there came a realization that a truly
great man had fallen.

Elder Andrews was laid to rest in a cemetery in
Basel, Switzerland. Through the fifty-four years of his
life, he did his best. He fought a good fight. He finished his course. He kept the faith. His crown of
righteousness is sure.

We invite you to view the complete
selection of titles we publish at:

www.TEACHServices.com

Please write or email us your praises, reactions, or
thoughts about this or any other book we publish at:

TEACH Services, Inc.
P U B L I S H I N G
www.TEACHServices.com • (800) 367-1844

P.O. Box 954
Ringgold, GA 30736

info@TEACHServices.com

TEACH Services, Inc., titles may be purchased in bulk for
educational, business, fund-raising, or sales promotional use.
For information, please e-mail:

BulkSales@TEACHServices.com

Finally, if you are interested in seeing
your own book in print, please contact us at

publishing@TEACHServices.com

We would be happy to review your manuscript for free.